Professionally Religious

by

Dare Blundell

Professionally Religious: The Spiritual Poverty of Spiritual
Leaders

©2015 by Dave Blundell

Scripture quotations are taken from the Holy Bible, New
Living Translation, copyright ©1996, 2004, 2007 by Tyndale
House Foundation. Used by permission of Tyndale House
Publishers, Inc., Carol Stream, Illinois 60188. All rights
reserved.

Published by Clovercroft Publishing, Franklin, Tennessee.

Published in association with Larry Carpenter of Christian
Book Services, LLC. www.christianbookservices.com

Cover and Interior Layout Design by Charlene Stinson
Cover Photograph by Robson Batista Digital Image
Edited by Gail Fallen

Printed in the United States of America

978-1-940262-93-2

"It's simple, easy to read, and provides bite-sized but theologically and professionally significant ideas to chew on. Reading this book is like performing diagnostics on your ministry life, philosophy, and theology. You don't have to agree with it all to still be prompted into some great self-reflection, learning, and ultimately, into a place where Jesus can pastor you."

Rev. Aaron D. Gerrard, Pastor
Ancaster Village Church

"I was reminded recently that humans have a tremendous capacity for self-deception. Professionally Religious is smelling salts for the soul of spiritual leaders."

Rev. Rob Ayer, Pastor
Crossroads Community Church

"If you're searching for a model of Christ-centered spiritual leadership, this book will help you. Dave Blundell challenges us to see spiritual leadership as a reflection of our relationship with Christ, instead of fulfilling the demands and expectations of others. Prepare to be convicted, stirred, and encouraged by this book."

Rev. Dave Van Roon, Pastor
Director of Clergy Health
Canadian Church of God Ministries

Foreword

Oh, the burden of being a leader today! Our authority is at an all-time low, our follow-ship is often fickle, our financial resources are dwindling and burnout abounds. One is required to ask: "Can these dead bones live?" Despite all the trials of ministry, we are seeing a renewal of Christian leadership. Dave's book will aid in this renewal of leadership. It is not for the faint of heart, or for those who are not secure in themselves. Hard questions are asked in love, just as Jesus came full of grace and truth. We often, however, want to hide from the truth; we are over sensitive and self-protecting. In Professionally Religious, Dave speaks prophetically to leaders and followers. Some will kill the prophet, some will banish him, others will be discipled by this prophet and live. Dave surgically removes the cancer from the Professionally Religious and enables the Holy Spirit to put flesh on these dry bones.

Two years ago, I had the privilege of going with Dave on

a trip to Cuba. I found in him a wise soul way beyond his years, with a generous heart, full of insight and a passion to support others in their ministry.

If your ministry is feeling stale, or you are not seeing the fruit you expected, or you are without vision, this book will stir you up, enable fruitfulness, and increase your vision.

Rt. Rev. Dr. Trevor H. Walters

Anglican Network in Canada
Suffragan Bishop for Western Canada

The LORD took hold of me, and I was carried away by the Spirit of the LORD to a valley filled with bones. He led me all around among the bones that covered the valley floor. They were scattered everywhere across the ground and were completely dried out. Then he asked me, "Son of man, can these bones become living people again?"

"O Sovereign LORD," I replied, "you alone know the answer to that."

Then he said to me, "Speak a prophetic message to these bones and say, 'Dry bones, listen to the word of the LORD! This is what the Sovereign LORD says: Look! I am going to put breath into you and make you live again! I will put flesh and muscles on you and cover you with skin. I will put breath into you, and you will come to life. Then you will know that I am the LORD.'"

So I spoke this message, just as he told me. Suddenly as I spoke, there was a rattling noise all across the valley. The bones of each body came together and attached themselves as complete skeletons. Then as I watched, muscles and flesh formed over the bones. Then skin formed to cover their bodies, but they still had no breath in them.

Then he said to me, "Speak a prophetic message to the winds, son of man. Speak a prophetic message and say, 'This is what the Sovereign LORD says: Come, O breath, from the four winds! Breathe into these dead bodies so they may live again.'"

So I spoke the message as he commanded me, and breath came into their bodies. They all came to life and stood up on their feet—a great army.

Table of Contents

Acknowledgements

I walked very carefully and extremely thoughtfully into these leadership thoughts. I don't propose to speak authoritatively or conclusively for or about spiritual leaders. I speak with leaders simply as a leader. As such, I thought it was extremely important to include a few Christ-following servant leaders into the process, as a review team, to help me communicate as effectively and as accurately as possible. I want to thank Trevor Walters, Rob Ayer, Charlene Stinson, Mike Bell, Aaron Gerrard, and Dave Van Roon for guiding and challenging me in many of these thoughts. I loved our discussions and your constructive feedback. You sifted and refined this message for it to have the greatest influence possible.

To the Evanow and Toews group...without your miraculous partnership...this would only be a document on a hard drive.

Thank you for teaching and transparently modeling spiritually vibrant servant leadership within the context of career ministry. You have been a Pastor, Professor, Preacher, Boss, Mentor and Friend to hundreds of leaders. I am incredibly thankful that I am one of the few that got to experience all of these in the past 25 years.

Preface: For the Love of Leaders

So many aspire to leadership—until they get there. From my experience and that of so many co-workers, this is especially true of spiritual leaders. Corporate leadership carries with it ideas of power, positions of respect, the authority to influence the agenda, and expectations of material reward that compensate the long hours and emotional load. Not so much in spiritual leadership. Balancing personal well-being and family responsibilities with the ever-growing expectations of people and kingdom accomplishment is a difficult job in itself. The expectations put on spiritual leaders are never ending: a Christ-like demeanor, a humble confidence, an entertaining and informing communicator, the quintessential counselor and—whatever else anyone needs.

The need to lead is all around us. It manifests itself when a group can't so little as decide on a place to eat or a person to say grace. The need to lead also manifests itself when children die before they should and stunned mourners look you in the eyes. While leadership action, or reaction, is always different with each situation, the same leadership responsibility is there when you open your eyes in the morning until you finally get to close them at night.

So why do it? Surely, there are easier ways to make a living. But the reality for those gifted with leadership, is that we can't not. In situations void of direction or movement, leaders can't often hold back the familiar compunction to act or speak whatever it takes to bring direction and cause action. People with leadership DNA built into their fibers can't help but lead. It wells up within them, reminding them that God's gifts are baked into the core of who they are. It is the same with all the other spiritual gifts Paul listed. Givers can't not give. Helpers can't not help. Teachers just find themselves teaching, planned or not.

Why? Because through all the wading around in the never-ending expectations of people, there are rare moments when leaders come alive and know exactly why they've been created and called for such a time as this. We live for those epic feelings that we are actually accomplishing something of value that will outlast us. An "Aha!" moment for your organization—an impassioned, clear, and convincing call to action that leads others to act—or a breakthrough change that you've been spending your life bringing about. They are more than just feelings of satisfaction or joy. They are defining experiences that make you know you are fully alive and fully in use as you were created to be.

The burdens of leadership never end, but neither do the opportunities for change. Leadership is hard, but the transformations that can be brought by Spirit-filled transformed leaders is the stuff that literally changes lives and even history. And it's for this hope of change that I first say I love leadership, and I love leaders. At times, as you read, you may not believe me. Because while I love leaders, I am, however, also terrified about the current climate of spiritual poverty and the cost

> **Leadership is hard, but the transformations that can be brought by Spirit-filled transformed leaders is the stuff that literally changes lives and even history.**

of failed spiritual leadership. Know that every hard word or thought I present has been—and will always be—first applied to me. Not because I am a masochist or a critic for critic's sake. (We have more than enough people critical of spiritual leaders today.) On the other hand, I can't help but be fixated on what the kingdom of God could look like on earth, as it is in heaven. That is the spirit and hope for which I feel so compelled to write these words.

Introduction

I was a freshman at Bible college when I first remember reading Matthew 23. I wasn't reading it for any of my classes at the time. I was reading in the dormitory stairwell. That's where I went to get away from people and spend time with Jesus. I remember it being the middle of winter. Frost had encased the emergency exit door and the window frame. The electric heater in the stairwell couldn't keep the Canadian prairie winter outside, so I had to bundle up to stay warm. But it was reading Matthew 23 that day that sent a chill through my soul.

God's direction in my life was extremely clear. The gifts and passions He gave me, the affirmation by people I trusted, and the natural inclinations of my heart all pointed to career leadership within the Church. In fact, God had completely reversed the direction of my life. My plan was to follow my dad and gradually grow into the family broadcasting business. I remember sitting in a small Methodist church one Sunday when we were visiting family. There were probably thirty-five people in the service that Sunday. Our family made up nine of them. As I listened to the pastor preach, I distinctly remember thanking God that I would never have to do what this poor man had to do. Getting paid next to nothing, studying the Bible, and speaking in public every week sounded worse than a prison sentence to me. I remember thanking God that I would never have to do any of those things. But I've discovered that it really is dangerous to say "never" to God.

Ironically, years later I was at BIBLE college. I was preparing to be a PASTOR. Getting a bachelor of THEOLOGY was the first step along the road to be ORDAINED. I was in the process of becoming professionally religious. And one unsuspecting day, I sat down and read Matthew 23:1-33:

Then Jesus said to the crowds and to his disciples: "The teachers of the law and the Pharisees sit in Moses' seat. So you must be careful to do everything they tell you. But do not do what they do, for they do not practice what they preach. They tie up heavy, cumbersome loads and put them on other people's shoulders, but they themselves are not willing to lift a finger to move them. Everything they do is done for people to see: They make their scripture prayer boxes wide and the tassels on their garments long; they love the place of honor at banquets and the most important seats in the synagogues; they love to be greeted with respect in the marketplaces and to be called 'Teacher' by others. But you are not to be called 'Teacher,' for you have one Teacher, and you are all brothers. And do not call anyone on earth 'father,' for you have one Father, and he is in heaven. Nor are you to be called 'Instructors,' for you have one Instructor, the Messiah. The greatest among you will be your servant. For those who exalt themselves will be humbled, and those who humble themselves will be exalted. Woe to you, teachers of the law and Pharisees, you hypocrites! You shut the door of the kingdom of heaven in people's faces. You yourselves do not enter, nor will you let those enter who are trying to. Woe to you, teachers of the law and Pharisees, you hypocrites! You travel over land and sea to win a single convert, and when you have succeeded, you make them twice as much a child of hell as you are. Woe to you, teachers of the law and Pharisees, you hypocrites! You give a tenth of your spices—mint, dill, and cumin. But you have neglected the more important matters of the law—justice, mercy, and faithfulness. You should have practiced the latter, without neglecting the former. You blind guides! You strain out a gnat but swallow a camel. Woe to you, teachers of the law and Pharisees, you hypocrites! You clean the outside of the cup and dish, but inside they are full of greed and self-indulgence. Blind Pharisee! First clean the inside of the cup and dish, and then the outside also will be clean. Woe to you, teachers of the law and Pharisees, you hypocrites! You are like whitewashed tombs, which look beautiful on the outside but on the inside are full of the bones of the dead and everything unclean. In the same way, on the outside you appear to people as righteous but on the inside you are full of hypocrisy and wickedness. Woe to you, teachers of the law and Pharisees, you hypocrites! You build tombs for the prophets and decorate the graves of the righteous. And you say, 'If we had lived in the days of our ancestors, we would not have taken part with them in shedding the blood of the prophets.' So you testify against yourselves that you are the descendants of those who murdered the prophets. Go ahead, then, and complete what your ancestors started! You snakes! You brood of vipers! How will you escape being condemned to hell?"

It rocked the core of my being. Here I was, preparing for the same career as those to whom Jesus directed this scathing rebuke. It was unfathomable that Jesus aimed this message at the professionally religious of His day! How dare He, just a carpenter, speak to the religious leaders and elite this way? Yet, Scripture records that during His three years of public ministry, Jesus was most antagonistic and most adversarial with the professionally religious. Jesus was constantly compassionate with broken people and constantly confrontational with the religious. And here I was, committing the rest of my life to become the latter?

I have spent the past twenty-five years either working as or working with the professionally religious all over the world. I was trained to be professionally religious. I have a bachelor's degree in theology and a master's degree in leadership. I am convinced that if Jesus were walking and talking in the flesh today, He'd be saying the same stuff that Matthew recorded in chapter 23. Throughout history, the Church repeatedly takes the concepts of the humble spiritual gift of servant leadership, and over time, morphs them into puffed up and self-serving positions for the professionally religious.

In Scripture, we could point to judges, kings, priests, Levites, Pharisees, and even the twelve disciples. In the two thousand years since Jesus, we could point to early leaders of what became the Catholic Church, Protestant reformers, new factions, splits, denominations, and para-church ministries–

example after example where God makes something sweet, fresh, and new out of old structures and religious institutions. Yet, over time, the new starts to be familiar, the familiar becomes the norm, and we lose the sweetness and the spiritual intimacy from which God did the new things. Human nature starts to creep in, and humble servant leaders begin the slide into self-serving positional propensities. Even more tragic, wherever her leaders go, so goes the Church. The spiritual poverty of the Western church points to spiritual heart failure in its leadership.

This is not another book about leadership. We have more than enough great books about leadership. This is a book that is first for the professionally religious, and second for those who follow us. This book started off as a series of entries in my personal journal and has been unintentionally written over a period of a few years. Over those years, the Holy Spirit challenged my core motives with Scripture, in prayer, and through many conversations and other writings. This is not about the skill or practice of leadership. This is all about being as vulnerable and open as I can be about my journey in professional religion and the motives of leadership toward the goal of being refined and filtered. I wrote this book because I am concerned for my own spiritual poverty as much as I am for that of spiritual leaders in general.

Such as journal entries do, some of these chapters will read in the recent past or present tense. Some will refer to other writers and leaders as they have impacted me, and I will be sure to credit the source where possible. Some of the chapters will read as conventional devotional thoughts, sermons, or blog posts, and some will read more like coffee table conversations. While this book is relatively short, it's not to be read quickly or in one sitting. I hope it takes you as long to read it as it did for me to write it. This book is also designed as a journal. Before each section, each chapter is listed and room is given for you to write a response. Jot down your thoughts as to how or if the chapter applies to you, and any changes you'd like to make in your life. You can also use this space to write your prayers to God or any Scripture that comes to mind. What you will write in this book is much more significant to me than anything I've written here.

What's my purpose with this book? Just as the book of Matthew was like a defibrillator on my professionally religious heart, my purpose and passion here is to reduce any appeal for career religion and to foster an ever-increasing hunger for servant-hearted intimacy with Jesus that can't help but transform the world around us. The counteragent of professional religion is spiritual vibrancy.

Before we get started, I want to admit that I will be primarily exploring the motives of the professionally religious. And by professionally religious, I am referring to those who have made a paid career out of spiritual leadership: leaders who are seen by followers as the "professionals." I want to look honestly at why the professionally religious do the things that we do. Motives are complex, and rarely do we do anything with just one in mind. We can have self-centered and selfless motives in any one decision at the same time. We all try to hide the self-centered motives and accentuate the selfless ones. I say this to fully acknowledge that the issues and deep places of the heart we will be exploring are not black and white. For all of us, there will be varying degrees to which we are challenged by these thoughts. There will also be some who have already been well refined in many of these areas.

Admittedly, I began my career professionally religious; I have been a recovering Pharisee ever since. God has had to jack hammer the foundation of my leadership values and pour the cement again. The following series of short thoughts reflect my conversations with God and with God's people as He continuously transforms my heart from being professionally religious to just—more like Jesus.

REFLECTION AND ACTION FOR THOSE WHO FOLLOW

This book is about the spiritual condition of spiritual leaders, and those who follow play a key role in the lives of leaders. Usually, alongside those in career spiritual leadership, there are boards, elders, deacons, and others who are biblically called to share the load of leading. The expectations of followers contribute heavily to the spiritual life or spiritual poverty of leaders. This first section speaks specifically to those led by leaders.

Each chapter in this section is listed with space following for you to write down thoughts, challenges, or actions you need to take. Read the chapter and then come back to this section to journal.

1. Looking For Reverend Perfect

_____

_____

_____

_____

_____

_____

_____

_____

_____

_____

_____

_____

2. Expectations

_____

_____

_____

_____

_____

_____

_____

_____

_____

_____

_____

_____

3. Pastors or Politicians

_____

_____

_____

_____

_____

_____

_____

_____

_____

_____

_____

_____

4. Selfish vs. Self-Care

_____

_____

_____

_____

_____

_____

_____

_____

_____

_____

_____

_____

5. *The Death of Personal Responsibility*

_____

_____

_____

_____

_____

_____

_____

_____

_____

_____

_____

_____

6. Hooked on Pablum

_____

_____

_____

_____

_____

_____

_____

_____

_____

_____

_____

_____

_____

7. So What Now For Followers

_____

_____

_____

_____

_____

_____

_____

_____

_____

_____

_____

_____

FOR THOSE WHO FOLLOW

CHAPTER ONE
looking for reverend perfect

I don't know of one great man of God in Scripture that would get hired by most churches today. He wouldn't fulfill the profile nor meet the expectations that people have of the professionally religious. Abraham helped himself to the house help when he didn't see how God was going to fulfill His promise. King David, a "man after God's own heart," wouldn't make the short list because of his murderous and adulterous past. Moses had a temper issue that caused him to kill an Egyptian as well as an apparent speech impediment that would have made him a terrible preacher. John the Baptist was simply too weird. Peter was a loud mouth who wasn't dependable and Paul, prior to his being transformed by Jesus, was guilty of killing believers and having little patience with people like Mark.

We live in a time and culture that is unfriendly and often hostile toward leaders, and in particular, spiritual leaders. Leaders can't be perfect enough to avoid the mistrust and antagonism of a hypercritical society. One of the many consequences of this pattern is that leaders find it very difficult to feel the freedom to be human. There is always someone who will be quick

> Leaders can't be perfect enough to avoid the mistrust and antagonism of a hypercritical society.

to point out a mistake, a difference with another leader, or a perceived weakness. Leaders find it difficult to be vulnerable, in part, because they don't feel it is safe. ("If people know what I really feel or think or struggle with, they will in some way reject me or my leadership.") People say they want their leaders to be transparent and vulnerable, but precious few can really handle that and what it means for them. Very few can extend the grace and safety that allows the professionally religious the freedom to let down their job-security shield so that they can also be followers of Jesus, and therefore, be on the same journey as other followers.

In addition to the personal insecurities of individual leaders, this lack of safety in community compounds the problem and leads leaders to present a whitewashed exterior, while the interior might be full of decay and neglect.

However, if the professionally religious work to move into a new reality of servant leadership, those few who are both led by us and also secure enough to handle our humanness become invaluable in creating places of emotional and spiritual safety. These are places where we don't have to worry about the security of our jobs—places where we can allow the Holy Spirit to go deeper within our own selves. If there are those who are up for the challenge of creating that kind of leader-friendly environment, you might just find yourselves on the front line of discovering that we may have more to give than we have ever had before--just like Abraham, Moses, David, John the Baptist, Peter, and Paul.

journal on page 2

CHAPTER TWO
expectations

Not that long ago, someone not so facetiously defined
leadership to me as "trying to disappoint people as slowly as
you possibly can." Not a motivating or inspiring definition,
but I smiled and completely understood the frustration.

There are so many armchair critics that have it all figured out
from the sidelines. Leadership appears so black and white
from the comfort of the couch. The game looks easy from
the bleachers. Most people think that their perspective is the
most accurate. They feel that their understanding is the most
right. And, therefore, if the leader was really "listening" they
would also see things and do things the same way.

In our self-centered and entitled generation, we have
ported consumerist expectations into our organizations and

churches. Many have the mindset that we give (pay), and we are therefore entitled to receive the services we prefer in the way in which we prefer them. If we don't get what we want, we vote with our wallets and our attendance. I especially love the anonymous "encouragement cards," or hastily sent emails—all meant to try to control from the sidelines and insist on having things "just the way you want them."

These consumerist expectations heavily contribute to the creation of the political in the professionally religious. Running around trying to find the fire behind the smoke, trying to make as many people as happy as possible, trying to create programming that is going to meet every "need" in the church, community, and world, reduces any leader's ability to have a focused impact.

> Let's step back and change our expectations of those who lead us and take responsibility for getting in the game ourselves.

Let's step back and change our expectations of those who lead us and take responsibility for getting in the game ourselves. Let me suggest two ways to practically "back off": Let go of your consumer expectations and build relationships with your leaders. Ask what their vision is and what their passions are, and commit to using your gifts to help them achieve what God is calling your community to be and do. Or...go somewhere else. It is not your church, no matter how long you've been attending or how much you've given. I'm guessing there are plenty of churches or organizations in driving distance that would align with your passion or preferences. Sometimes, the most loving and selfless thing you can do is make yourself less.

journal on page 3

CHAPTER THREE
pastors or politicians

A few times in my professionally religious career when our church considered hiring a pastor, I sat in on these town-hall type meetings. Maybe you've been a part of something similar. The candidate speaks for a while, and then everyone who shows up can ask questions. Typically, people ask the candidate how much he or she values the area of church life that is the most important to them.

"How important is children's ministry to you?"

"What is your value for Senior's visitation?"

"How much of the Sunday service do you give to the worship?"

"What is your perspective on the importance of the men's

ministry?"

"We have always been a missions-giving church; what value do you place on missions in your leadership?"

In each of the responses, the candidate has to carefully word his or her answers to try to communicate that he or she values all of it without giving the impression that they will be able to prioritize all of it in the first week or month or even year. In every case, these town hall meetings become identical to political Q & A meetings, with the prospective leader giving carefully-worded statements to try and secure as many "Amens" and votes as possible to get elected.

Then, when that leader is hired, appointed, or elected, so begin the expectations that he or she will be everything to everyone. So also begins the rat race of over-commitment that will eventually become burnout. What happens is that

> ...people equate the pastor or leader's time and attendance at their program with his or her value of that specific ministry.

people equate the pastor or leader's time and attendance at

their program with his or her value of that specific ministry. Without giving any real thought to the rest of the leader's life and schedule, they assume that if the leader doesn't come to what they value the most, then he or she must not really care about it. In twenty years of church ministry, I've seen and heard it over and over...and over.

"The pastor does not come to our 55+ events. And he hasn't visited my aging mother in months. He doesn't care about seniors."

"The pastor didn't come to the missions' service. He doesn't really care about missions in this church."

"The pastor didn't come to the men's golf tournament. He doesn't make men's ministry a priority like he said he would."

"Our pastor hasn't preached on prayer for so long. He hasn't come to a prayer meeting in months. He does not value prayer."

In short—grow up! These statements sound like the playground whining of children. Of course your pastor or leader values all of these things, or they wouldn't be your pastor. Give some thought to the reality that this one person cannot be at everything all the time AND have a healthy family life AND have a healthy personal walk with Jesus, which, by the way, is the most important thing he or she should be giving his or her time to.

journal on page 4

CHAPTER FOUR
selfish vs. self-care

Very closely related to the previous chapter is another area so dangerously ignored by those who follow the professionally religious. Along with the expectation that leaders attend or lead most of the programs of the church in order to prove their value for them, is the probability that the leader will quickly neglect their relationship with Jesus. If pastors have a heart for their people, and they also battle with the need for approval, it is so perilously easy to relegate that which should be their first priority to something much further down the list.

I would go so far as to say that when a leader says, "No, I'm sorry, I'm not going to spend time with you or attend that event, I need to get away and be with the Lord" or "I can't commit to that because I have a family commitment" or "I feel I need to get away with God for an extended period for Sabbath and study," many will accuse the leader of being selfish. Many will say, "Well...I don't get to do that in my job!"

That evaluation and judgment is usually based out of jealously, a terrible understanding of what Scripture says is the role of a teacher or shepherd or prophet, as well as a full acceptance of North American society's value system. What these followers are judging as selfish is actually self-care and is the most valuable thing leaders can do to serve their people.

The most valuable thing followers can do to help their leaders not become professionally religious is to make sure, above anything else on their job descriptions, that they prioritize time spent in prayer and time fostering their relationship with Jesus. The healthier they are personally, the more powerful they are publicly.

> The healthier they are personally, the more powerful they are publicly.

I'm currently sitting on a flight home. This one started just like every single flight I've ever taken—with the safety demonstration. Although it is the same perfunctory information every time, there is always one part that catches my attention because it seems counterintuitive. I understand why they tell us to do it but it still seems...selfish. It's the part about putting on the oxygen mask. "Please put on your own mask before helping others." My son is sitting beside me right now, and if those things fell out of the ceiling panel, I'd be awfully tempted to put his mask on before mine. But here's the thing, I can't help him to breathe if I'm not.

I think you get the point.

journal on page 5

CHAPTER FIVE
the death of personal responsibility

Do you ever notice when people talk about an unwelcome situation in their lives that it's usually someone else's fault? The situation I would rather not be dealing with is my boss' fault for not giving me enough information. It's my wife's fault for not understanding me. It's my pastor's fault for not doing what I told him to do. It's my teacher's fault for being so strict. It's my colleague's fault for not meeting a deadline. It's the kids' fault for not obeying. And it is always, somehow, the government's fault.

Critical, fault-finding, judgmental and blaming attitudes are subtle forms of self-preservation that enable me to absolve myself of personal responsibility for my actions. They enable me to feel better about myself compared with other people;

no matter how right I think I am. This thinking gives me false license to ignore my own issues.

You rarely hear people say, "You know...the situation is the way it is because I've made some stupid choices." Or, you seldom hear people say, "Wow...did I ever screw that up!" We, being prideful, can't handle the thought of admitting that we were wrong or of showing people the reality that things are the way they are because of choices we made or didn't make. It's much more convenient to blame someone else for the unfortunate situations we may find ourselves in. It's much more comforting to live in a dream world, where we are victims of someone else's actions. And while there are victims and perpetrators in this world, the reality is that

> ...we, individually, are the common denominator in all of our problems.

we, individually, are the common denominator in all of our problems. No matter how much we may feel that our present situation is the culmination of a past we did not choose, the fact remains that our future reality and perspective are completely our responsibility.

journal on page 6

CHAPTER SIX
hooked on pablum

As long as we continue with this unbiblical idea that we pay the minister to minister, the North American church will continue to flounder in spiritual apathy and mediocrity. The idea carries the expectation that we just show up to the table and pay someone to shove food into our mouths. One consequence is that we don't know how to really feed ourselves and take responsibility for our own spiritual nourishment. We stay as infants–totally reliant on the adults to break down the tough bits of our food and make it as palatable and as easy to swallow as possible.

While Scripture does teach that teachers should teach, it also teaches that we need to move beyond milk onto solid foods. We have never lived in a time when it's more possible to take responsibility for our own spiritual nutrition; yet so many of us still leave that up to the professionally religious.

Paying the professional also tends to cause followers to default to expecting that we just—follow. We act like it's the hired help who is responsible for doing the hard work of reaching people, discipling, managing conflict, or whatever else it is we are uncomfortable doing. Oh, we may pitch in and help set up chairs every once in a while, but for the most part we leave the heavy lifting of the serious work to the professionally religious.

Scripture gives us so much vision for how God intends His kingdom to function. We are told we are a body, each with their own job with Him as the head. No one part of the body is any more important than the other or has any more responsibility than the other or is meant to be more professional than the other. Ephesians 4 and 1 Corinthians 12 talk about how ridiculous it is for us to treat one member of the body like it's up to them alone to get the job done. Here's the biblical and practical bottom line; the Church will not be effective, and the world

> ...the Church will not be effective, and the world will not be reached, by just a professional few.

will not be reached, by just a professional few.

Not only does this fee-paying and observing mentality leave the Church stalled in obscurity and passivity, it also breeds an environment that causes followers to think that they get to have things their way. While Jesus calls spiritual leaders to be servants and not professionally religious, this does not mean it gives followers a license to treat them like slaves.

journal on page 7

CHAPTER SEVEN
so-what now for followers?

As I said in the introduction, where our leaders go, so go our organizations. There is much responsibility on the hearts of spiritual leaders. If a church, an organization, or business is failing or stalled or ineffective, I firmly believe it comes back to something failing, stalled, or ineffective in the leadership or leadership teams. I've heard lots of leaders blaming followers for not following, and while there are always plenty of stubborn sheep in a flock, people will only be able to go as far as their leaders are willing to go themselves. When there is a presenting problem, the first place to look is at leadership.

However, the culture of a group and the attitudes of the unofficial influential can have an organization spinning for years in mediocrity and ineffectiveness. We see this repeatedly in Scripture, in the nation of Israel, and I've seen it repeatedly in churches and organizations today. Followers are constantly complaining about their leaders and calling it "accountability." Talking about the leader and not to the leader and calling it "sharing a frustration." Engaging in after-church gossip and judgment and calling it "voicing a concern."

> **Followers are constantly complaining about their leaders and calling it accountability.**

But what do you do if someone who leads you fits the classic biblical description of the professionally religious? Understanding that you are led by a human with weaknesses, how can you handle that without morphing into the classic description of complaining, cranky sheep?

I want to give some practical suggestions, or coaching, that might help both those who are led by spiritual servant leaders and also those who are led by leaders who have become professionally religious.

More than everything else on a leader's job description, make sure he or she has the freedom to prioritize his or her relationship with God without feeling like he or she is not doing his or her job. I think this is the most important thing anyone can do to help prevent spiritual leaders from becoming professionally religious. When leaders are spent, empty, and void of personal spiritual life, they are still paid to lead, preach, teach, inspire, pray, and counsel. And when they continually give out of that emptiness, professional religion develops and starts to take over the life of a leader. Out of a need to protect an income and an image, perpetuating a job takes priority over a life of ministry. Ask how their soul is. Make sure they have extended times of retreat or Sabbath and that it does not have to count as vacation. The counteragent against professional religion is spiritual vibrancy.

Get to know your leaders and ask them to help you understand their actions and decisions. Without knowing the motives or the intent behind decisions, it's easy to assume you know what they are. Ask questions; don't make statements. Give them the benefit of the doubt. They have just as much a desire to effectively reach people as anyone else in the church or organization.

Don't enable gossip or complaining about your leaders, especially if people haven't first talked to the leader about the way they feel. People love the ability to say what they want about leaders without having to be accountable for their words. We are far too timid to say to each other something like, "Hold on. Have you first shared your feelings with the leader?" People want to feel validated in their disappointments and frustrations, and the easiest way to feel that is to find someone who might feel the same way and talk about it. There are always more perspectives than yours, no matter how convinced you are.

Find out if the organization has a staff review process in place. If they don't, encourage there be one. If they do, trust it. Is the issue you feel strongly about an issue of wrong versus right or an issue of preference? If you feel it's truly an issue of wrong versus right, and the leader repeatedly dismisses you, take your concern to another leader in the organization. If a leader can't handle being questioned or is always dismissive of evaluation that comes in the right spirit, the leader has succumbed to professional religion, and hard decisions need to be made.

Pray for your leaders, and trust that God can speak to them. No matter how much you feel that your issue is burning and just must be raised, do you trust that God is aware of the situation? Don't you think that He can raise an issue if it's that crucial? As a follower, I sometimes have not understood why leaders have led the way that they have. Some decisions have been head-shakers for me. But at the end of the day, I have had to make the choice to shut up, and let the Holy Spirit be the Holy Spirit.

If you just can't support the leader or the direction of the church or organization in which you are involved, consider leaving gracefully and find an organization or church where you can. Leaving gracefully will cause less damage than staying and causing division within the church or organization by your inability to fully support the leadership. There are many brands and varieties of churches. God is at work through so many of them to establish His kingdom. It is unhealthy ownership to feel that you must hang onto one particular local church regardless of the divisive consequences.

Be extremely careful in thinking that you'll be able to change passions, vision, leadership style, and gifting by persuasively or continually confronting your fellow congregants with your firmly held convictions. I've never seen it happen. I've only seen it frustrate the leader and follower more and more.

Think about the reality that in any organization or church, there are hundreds or thousands of people evaluating the leadership against their expectations, reasonable or not. The leaders are constantly working to juggle these expectations among the myriad of others they have to consider. Spiritual leaders need other leaders who understand that a minister's job is not solely to minister. We need people to understand that it wasn't until hundreds of years after Christ that we constructed the difference between the lay leadership and the clergy. And, for hundreds of years, we've perpetuated the idea that there are one or two that "minister" and the rest of us show up, observe, and pay the professionally religious to be professional. And that lets us off the hook from believing that we are all priests and ministers who can and should all work and serve in His kingdom.

journal on page 8

Reflection and Action for Those Who Lead

Self-awareness is such a rare but needed quality for a leader. It is easy to think about how these types of issues apply to other people or another group, but I encourage you to use them as your own checklist. Not every chapter will apply to you, but likely some will. Please be reflective and self-examining as you read. The spiritual condition and resurgence of the Western Church lies most heavily on those who provide it leadership. Nothing is more important for advancement of the kingdom than the work of the Spirit in the lives of those who lead.

Each chapter in this section is listed with space following for you to write down thoughts, challenges, or actions you need to take. Read the chapter and then come back to this section to journal.

8. Follow The Servant

_____

_____

_____

_____

_____

_____

_____

_____

_____

_____

_____

_____

9. *The Ability To Walk Past a Need*

_____

_____

_____

_____

_____

_____

_____

_____

_____

_____

_____

10. Santa Claus or Coach

_____

_____

_____

_____

_____

_____

_____

_____

_____

_____

_____

_____

11. Self-Emptying Love

---

12. Food Court Leadership

_____

_____

_____

_____

_____

_____

_____

_____

_____

_____

_____

_____

13. The Shoulds & Shouldn'ts of Religion

_____

_____

_____

_____

_____

_____

_____

_____

_____

_____

_____

14. *The Need For Approval*

_____

_____

_____

_____

_____

_____

_____

_____

_____

_____

_____

_____

15. *The Infection Spreads*

_____

_____

_____

_____

_____

_____

_____

_____

_____

_____

_____

_____

_____

16. The Big Deal About Buildings

_____

_____

_____

_____

_____

_____

_____

_____

_____

_____

_____

_____

17. *Size Does Matter*

_____

_____

_____

_____

_____

_____

_____

_____

_____

_____

_____

_____

18. *The Scariest Thing Jesus Said*

_____

_____

_____

_____

_____

_____

_____

_____

_____

_____

_____

_____

19. For Whose Benefit Do I Lead?

_____

_____

_____

_____

_____

_____

_____

_____

_____

_____

_____

_____

20. *A Culture of Yes*

_____

_____

_____

_____

_____

_____

_____

_____

_____

_____

_____

_____

21. Contemporary Legalism

_____

_____

_____

_____

_____

_____

_____

_____

_____

_____

_____

_____

22. *No Leadership Without Real Empathy*

_____

_____

_____

_____

_____

_____

_____

_____

_____

_____

_____

_____

_____

23. Hypocrites and Blind Guides

_____

_____

_____

_____

_____

_____

_____

_____

_____

_____

_____

_____

24. Critical and Judgmental

_____

_____

_____

_____

_____

_____

_____

_____

_____

_____

_____

_____

25. Territorialism in the Kingdom

_____

_____

_____

_____

_____

_____

_____

_____

_____

_____

_____

_____

26. Fighting Over the How

_____

_____

_____

_____

_____

_____

_____

_____

_____

_____

_____

_____

27. The Wheat in the Chaff

28. *The Temptation to Be Relevant*

_____

_____

_____

_____

_____

_____

_____

_____

_____

_____

_____

_____

29. The Temptation to Be Spectacular

_____

_____

_____

_____

_____

_____

_____

_____

_____

_____

_____

_____

30. The Temptation to Be Powerful

_____

_____

_____

_____

_____

_____

_____

_____

_____

_____

_____

_____

_____

31. The Temptation of Title

_____

_____

_____

_____

_____

_____

_____

_____

_____

_____

_____

_____

32. The Temptation to Control

_____

_____

_____

_____

_____

_____

_____

_____

_____

_____

_____

_____

_____

33. The Temptation of Entitlement

_____

_____

_____

_____

_____

_____

_____

_____

_____

_____

_____

_____

34. *The Temptation to be Better*

_____

_____

_____

_____

_____

_____

_____

_____

_____

_____

_____

_____

35. The Temptation of Busy

_____

_____

_____

_____

_____

_____

_____

_____

_____

_____

_____

_____

36. The Temptation of Perpetual Mediocrity

_____

_____

_____

_____

_____

_____

_____

_____

_____

_____

_____

_____

37. Doing No Favors

_____

_____

_____

_____

_____

_____

_____

_____

_____

_____

_____

_____

38. Heart-Check Questions For The Professionally Religious

_____

_____

_____

_____

_____

_____

_____

_____

_____

_____

_____

_____

39. A Servant Leader's Prayer

_____

_____

_____

_____

_____

_____

_____

_____

_____

_____

_____

_____

_____

40. So—What Now For the Professionally Religious?

_____

_____

_____

_____

_____

_____

_____

_____

_____

_____

_____

_____

FOR THOSE WHO LEAD

CHAPTER EIGHT
follow the servant

Matthew 3:13-17

Then Jesus went from Galilee to the Jordan River to be baptized by John. But John tried to talk him out of it. "I am the one who needs to be baptized by you," he said, "so why are you coming to me?" But Jesus said, "It should be done, for we must carry out all that God requires." So John agreed to baptize him. After his baptism, as Jesus came up out of the water, the heavens were opened, and he saw the Spirit of God descending like a dove and settling on him. And a voice from heaven said, "This is my dearly loved Son, who brings me great joy."

The first recorded words spoken by Jesus were that He needed to be obedient and be baptized. John is acutely and understandably uncomfortable baptizing the Son of God. So much so that he protests at first and says, in effect, "Wait a minute! This baptism doesn't feel right. This is all backwards. You're the Messiah. You're the boss here. It should be you baptizing me."

No one would've questioned anything if Jesus had taken over and started baptizing people, especially after hearing a big voice from the heavens proclaiming He was God's son. John would've been happy to step out of the way and let the "boss" take over. But, no; while that's what the professionally religious might do, that's not what a servant does.

This was Jesus' public debut. This would set the tone. It would establish expectations and make first impressions on what the kingdom of God would look like. You'd think a healing or raising someone from the dead might set a better precedent displaying the power of this new kingdom. But this was kick-off Sunday...the big reveal. This was when God Himself was going to speak audibly and introduce the new King.

What happened instead was a lot less regal. Assuming others were there to be baptized; the Son of God got in line with the sinners. Jesus' first great act was one of great humility. He submitted Himself to being baptized. Even though He had no need to be cleansed of anything, He humbled Himself to baptism and told John that He was there to be obedient. Jesus didn't need to be baptized, but He did need to be a servant and an example. He wasn't willing to call people to do anything He wouldn't be willing to submit to Himself, a core value that is seldom practiced by the professionally religious.

The professionally religious might talk a good sermon about servant leadership and being an example, but many really like the front seats, the big offices, the titles on the business cards, and the image of being in charge of something. The servant is the first to get there and the last to leave, but the

> Jesus didn't need to be baptized, but He did need to be a servant and an example.

professionally religious are addicted to being the last to get there and the first to leave.

On the one hand, I love that Jesus kicked everything off with this powerful act of humility. It set the contrast that this kingdom was the antithesis of the religion that was passing as standard. On the other hand, I am constantly convicted that my professionally religious predisposition is shot down when the invitation is given to follow the Servant.

journal on page 40

the ability to walk past a need

One of the things I envy the most about Jesus' leadership is all that He didn't do. My heart is constantly wrung out by the enormity of the need around me and the finite amount of time and emotional resources that I have. Many professionally religious have a hard time deciding which people they are not going to help and an even harder time wrestling with how to make that decision. For three years, Jesus was constantly surrounded by large groups of people. The version of the Bible I read uses the word "crowds" more than 150 times in the Gospels. In most of these, Jesus is healing, feeding or preaching to those crowds.

I often think, though, for all that Jesus did, how did He decide what not to do? How did He decide what need not to meet or whom not to heal or what not to preach? In many of these very public situations, there are stories of Him healing people–but not many, and certainly not everyone. There had to be others in the crowds who were sick or had children who were suffering from one thing or another; how did Jesus decide what He was going to do and what He wasn't?

This issue drives me crazy in a world so full of need. I've walked in leper colonies and garbage villages. I've led food distributions at refugee camps where there are always more hungry families than sacks of rice and beans. I've helped at medical camps where the lineup of sick children is always longer than a day. It doesn't matter if we're talking about the poorest nation in the world or the school my children attend, there is always more need for more time and resources than I have to give.

Why didn't Jesus ever tell us how to make the decision of how to walk past a need? He obviously walked past many needs that He didn't meet. Why didn't the disciples ever ask Him? Was Jesus OK with healing one person and knowing that there were many in the crowds that were still sick? Did He stay awake at night wondering how to impact more people? Because Jesus is silent on this one, and because this is something caring leaders think about a lot, I'm going to take my best shot at it.

Maybe it's way simpler than I think. Could it be that Jesus simply responded to whatever need He felt the most compelled to meet at that moment? If He is one with His Father as He claimed (John 10:30), then I think we can assume that His heart was led to do what the Father wanted done. If His heart was led to heal someone, that person was healed. If His heart was led to feed people, they were fed.

If we are on a journey of becoming one with our Father as Jesus was, then maybe we can confidently do the same. Instead of getting all twisted up in decisions made complex by who has the most need, who has the best pitch, or what will be the political fallout of not meeting a need, maybe it's as simple as doing what your heart is most led to do. Maybe we need to realize that if Jesus didn't assume responsibility for meeting every need before Him, neither should we. Instead, we have a responsibility to listen to our hearts in the face of all the need that is before us and respond to what we feel most compelled. If Jesus is truly the Lord of my heart, I can assume He is leading me to where He wants my heart to go.

I was brought up in a religious culture that taught me that I can't and shouldn't trust my feelings and emotions in the process of hearing God. We hear pious statements about the need to "find out what God wants" apart from our feelings; but could it be that God communicates and directs us, in large part, by our feelings?

In all of the references to crowds in the Gospels, four of those references talk about Jesus getting away from the crowds to be with His Father. Even He needed to be away from the "many" to be with the "One" so that He had something to give to the many again. So, at the very least, we need to follow that example and make sure we also get away and foster our "oneness" with Him. As we do that, let's confidently do whatever it is we feel led to do, but then let's also confidently leave the rest to Him.

> Even He needed to be away from the many to be with the One so that He had something to give to the many again.

journal on page 41

CHAPTER TEN
santa claus or coach

Please allow me an oversimplification. There are two models of leadership I've been thinking about: leading as Santa and leading as a coach.

As warm and fuzzy as the concept of Santa Claus is, his is a terrible leadership style! The idea that there is one main man at the top, with hundreds of little helpers making him look good, would be considered bad leadership even by bad leaders. Santa is a larger-than-life person. Everyone knows his name, and he's the one who gets the credit and the adulation by people all over the world. He rides in with a slick suit, and everyone thinks it's because of him that children everywhere get toys at Christmas. We never hear anything about the leadership team or structure, let alone a succession plan.

I love to coach my son's baseball teams. In another life,

I'd coach and play baseball with kids all day. A coach, I've learned, is a totally different leader than Santa. It is the players who are seen as the stars by everyone. The coach stays on the bench or in the dugout and is rarely in the spotlight. The coach's job is done mostly out of the sight of the crowds and the fans. Many people don't even know the coach's name, because his job is to make the players known. Most often, the players are actually better at playing the game than the coach is. For a coach, the point of the organization is a team, and not the individual.

> We like the idea of empowerment, delegation, and servanthood, but we like the feeling of the spotlight better.

While every leader would probably agree that being like a coach is better than being like Santa, it is a lot harder to lead and live like a coach. We have to fight our self-focused nature to take Santa-like credit in our conversations and leadership. We like the idea of empowerment, delegation, and servanthood, but we like the feeling of the spotlight, the credit, and the kudos.

Being like a coach or like Santa is not a one-time leadership decision. It is likely a decision we need to make multiple times a day when we examine the motives of our seemingly small decisions and actions. Let's put on the filter and ask the question, "In this action, decision, or statement, am I trying to act as the big man in a red suit, or the one on the sideline wearing the same uniform as everyone else on the field?"

journal on page 42

CHAPTER ELEVEN
self-emptying love

Truly leading like Jesus starts by applying self-emptying love.
However, all too often, what I end up practicing instead is self-promotion. Self-promotion compares myself to others and looks for ways to evaluate myself by the words and actions of others. Self-promotion looks for ways to be valued and stroked. Self-promotion defaults to seeing everyone's reality through the lens of my own experiences and passing value judgment based on my own values. Self-promotion is desperate to find ways to avoid looking wrong, and to do

> Self-promotion can even be temporarily masked in public attempts to display humility and service for the purpose of trying to leave a self-emptying perception.

so, to point out the imperfections of others. Self-promotion can even be temporarily masked in public attempts to display humility and service for the purpose of trying to leave a self-emptying impression. Such self-promotion might be the most dangerous of all. Self-hatred is often a subtler means by which we attain self-promotion and the reason we use to over examine what people think of us.

Real self-emptying love finds a greater joy in considering the reality of others more valuable than my own. Self-emptying love enables me to see the inner needs of people through their sometimes confusing and even hurtful actions. This love then compels me to attend to those needs in such a way that people feel they are greater and more valuable in my presence. Self-emptying love doesn't fear being wrong or even looking wrong, and therefore, doesn't necessitate me pointing out other people's faults or looking for "I told you so" opportunities. Self-emptying love doesn't look to turn the conversation back to myself, but rather encourages people to dive even deeper into their stories.

In the world of "churchianity," we leaders learn quickly how to put on a plastic religious show. We know how to both speak and look outwardly spiritual. Much more difficult is real

Christ-likeness. Real Christ-likeness is concerned much more about the true attitude of the heart, from which the actions of Christ become mirrored in my life and are reflected to the world.

And here is the path to self-emptying leadership.

Philippians 2:5-8
Your attitude should be the same that Christ Jesus had. Though he was God, he did not demand and cling to his rights as God. He made himself nothing; he took the humble position of a slave appeared in human form. And in human form he obediently humbled himself even further by dying a criminal's death on a cross.

journal on page 43

food court leadership

I'm sitting in the food court, in an airport. It's a typical small food court, with a couple of big name favorites and a couple of eateries I've never heard of. People are wandering in... stopping...scanning the menus above the counters and slowly making their way over to the place they prefer. Some families come in and head in a few different directions because the parents are interested in Starbucks, and the kids make a beeline for Burger King. And once they get their food they all come together and eat in the middle, and unless you look carefully, it's actually hard to tell where people have been to eat.

I wish the Church were more like a food court.

The five different places in the food court aren't arguing which place to eat is better. The manager at Pizza Hut isn't standing out front preaching that the food served there is the only REAL food. The manager at the Italian place isn't wandering over to those in line at Burger King subtly telling them that his food is more relevant. The young guitar-playing Starbucks manager isn't out front saying that they serve lattes, and the other places serve bad coffee. In fact, all of these places are sharing all the resources they can. They share seats, garbage cans, cleaning staff, bathrooms, and parking lots. Why duplicate resources that they can share? That way, more money, time, and human resources can be spent on serving hungry people. The end goal is the same. People are getting fed before they wing off to wherever they are going. The process of getting fed is only about personal preference.

The parallel is hopefully obvious. Sunday school or kids clubs, music style, programming, staffing, sermons, curriculum, and youth groups are all preferences in the process of getting fed. But far too often, we want to make our particular preferences sacred and say to everyone else that the way we do things is THE most right—that our way of spiritually feeding people is THE most right way to feed people. We typically make our "normal" the most right, and while we wouldn't outright say it, we judgmentally walk around like the other places to eat just aren't quite as good as ours. This both screams of religious institutional arrogance and reduces people's view of who God is and what He does.

I think that the food court has a lot to teach the Church.

journal on page 44

the "shoulds" & "shouldn'ts" of religion

"Should." I hate that word. It says (in a whiny sort of way) "I don't want to...but I guess I must." It's the classic feel and language of what everyone hates about religion. Obligation. Duty. Onus. Expectation. The heavy burden of trying to keep a deity happy is full of "shoulds." Living up to man-made interpretations or community expectations is full of "shoulds." We often worry about what we should or shouldn't do with our moral choices. We agonize over what people will think of our religious flavor and us.

We say yes to all of the activities the church has planned because we think we should. "I should do this" is most often a statement motivated by guilt or a focus on what our leaders will think of us if we don't do what they would like us to do.

Should–motivated behavior assumes God will be happier with us if we do things we don't want to do. Acting on the basis of what we should do can also make us feel pridefully better about ourselves—and also better than the people who aren't doing what we are. Doing "should" stuff can make us look like a martyr and fosters spiritual pride, the most dangerous form of pride I've seen. Saying yes based on the "should system" mostly just makes us busy and empty, not effective and fulfilled.

And then there are the "shouldn'ts." We spend far too much time trying to get people to want to sin less. I also think we spend far too much time trying to sell people on the idea of wanting to be more committed to their faith and living it out. Even the very word "religion" is thick with a prescribed behavior-driven lifestyle.

The "shoulds" of religion are not why Jesus came. We don't need the "shoulds" of religion to earn our way onto God's honor role. I strongly believe that "shoulds" don't need to factor into our decision-making. Jesus didn't come to show us a better way that we should live. Focusing on the "shoulds" and the "shouldn'ts" of religion displays a lack of trust in the indwelling Holy Spirit to guide us into what He wants us to say yes or no to. It causes us to look for a formula for our faith rather than a relationship with Jesus.

When we continuously act out of the place of emptiness or void of intimacy with God, our lives are ruled by "shoulds," and once again, we have religion.

I believe that it is possible to live in such a relationship with Jesus, experiencing such intimacy that He forms our desires. And therefore, whatever we most want to choose at any one time is what He most wants for us. I also believe that we can live in such intimacy with Jesus that He places His desires in our hearts. Which means, we don't have to worry about the sins we shouldn't commit, because we won't even want to sin.

When we blow it—and we will—when we do stuff we know we shouldn't do, we can thank God that He is stirring something within us that agrees we've missed His best for us. Then we can also thank God that He loves us as we are and not as we should be.

journal on page 45

the need for approval

The need for approval is so basic and fundamental to being human. Most of us avoid being rejected like the plague, and we do almost anything to establish and preserve our worth in the eyes of others. Leader or not, we clamber up the ladder of value feeling better about ourselves with each rung. While this is common and healthy, it's particularly dangerous and destructive in leaders.

A subtle subtext of insecure leadership is the temptation to be popular: to be wanted, to be accepted. By reason of our complete acceptance by God, we have the means to be secure without the accolades of people. However, the professionally religious are as susceptible as anyone to adopt whatever agenda or speech will derive the greatest amount of personal approval.

We're rarely aware of how the need to be liked and the addiction to control what people think of us can affect our actions and decisions. For leaders, the symptoms include overcommitting, the inability to say no, changing our convictions based on whom we're talking to, not taking a stand, telling people what they want to hear, trying to act like someone we're not, being crushed by criticism, and the inability to handle disagreement or conflict, just to name a few.

If we really understood who we are, that we are chosen to be children of God, appointed as His representatives, gifted uniquely, and called for a time and purpose, we can be free from the chains that come from the secret hidden mission of striving for approval. In light of our outright and secure acceptance by God, why is there any temptation to crave the acceptance of people? We don't have to work to gain the approval of Jesus. We already have it. So why do we care about the approval of other insecure people?

In additional to personal insecurity, I believe that our need for approval is directly tied to our need for a paycheck. Along with our model for funding churches and organizations, the professionally religious can be in a constant conflict of interest between our desire to lead with risk-taking boldness and the fact that people vote for approval with their wallets. The typical result is that the professionally religious always have job security as our filter when we speak and lead. Our model of funding often creates political leaders rather than spiritual leaders. While it is biblical to fund the ministries of people whose gifts and calling align with career ministry, it is also clear that money should never be a motivating factor. Until we have spiritual leaders who lead unencumbered by the security of a paycheck, churches and organizations will continue to exist only for those already on the inside. To do otherwise will take leaders who trust God for both their personal and financial security.

> Until we have spiritual leaders who lead unencumbered by the security of a paycheck, churches and organizations will continue to exist only for those already on the inside.

While our security in Christ is easy to understand factually, to consistently act on it is incredibly difficult. However, the greater we are immersed in this truth, the freer we are from the prison of needing approval.

journal on page 46

CHAPTER FIFTEEN
the infection spreads

It did not take long for the disciples to become infected with professional religion. Near the end of their time with Jesus, there were signs that even they started to present some of the symptoms. I wonder if Jesus was disappointed to see some of the symptoms present in the leadership of these men with whom He had just spent the last three years.

Matthew 26:6-13
Meanwhile, Jesus was in Bethany at the home of Simon, a man who had previously had leprosy. While he was eating, a woman came in with a beautiful alabaster jar of expensive perfume and poured it over his head. The disciples were indignant when they saw this. "What a waste!" they said. "It could have been sold for a high price and the money given to the poor." But Jesus, aware of this, replied, "Why criticize

this woman for doing such a good thing to me? You will always have the poor among you, but you will not always have me. She has poured this perfume on me to prepare my body for burial. I tell you the truth, wherever the Good News is preached throughout the world, this woman's deed will be remembered and discussed."

Over the three years of Jesus' time with these guys, it looks as if they had started to develop certain roles and responsibilities within the team. Their gifts had been used and were evident to each other. They must have had some systems in place—some dealt with finances and some with other details—some were the preachers, and some were counselors. They had ways they did things and ways they didn't. We read in places that their personalities came into play. And in this situation, it says "they," as in plural, got indignant at this use of money. It didn't fit with their plan. This was not how they did things. They already had traditions, and in this case, the perfume was to be sold and the money given to the poor: a good thing, right? Normally, yes, but in this case, tradition had become a symptom of professional religion.

The disciples were starting to act like the Pharisees. They

were missing the point. The moment the protection and the perpetuation of the program becomes more important than the people involved, you've got professional religion again. They were angry that this perfume had been wasted on the worship of Jesus when it could have been sold to support a program. I think this is another hallmark of professional religion, when worship is relegated further down the priority list because we are so consumed with running our programs.

> The moment the protection and the perpetuation of the program becomes more important than the people involved, you've got professional religion again.

Again, Jesus zeros in on the counteragent of professional religion. He points out that we will always have programs to run, but the priority is always fostering intimacy with Him. As important as Jesus tells us it is to feed the poor, this woman's adoration of Him and His response to it shows what is of greatest importance.

journal on page 47

the big deal about buildings

Before embarking on a building project, I think ministry and church leadership should ask themselves some hard questions. Gone are the days of "if you build it they will come." I think I've heard all the arguments and reasons that people should support a building or capital project. We usually appeal to something outreach related. Something like, "We want to use our building for outreach in the community, so we need to do this building project." That might sound altruistic, but I have never heard of a church growing because it has a really nice or newly renovated building. I have never heard someone's conversion story go like this: "I turned my life over to Jesus because the church on Third Avenue has a nice building."

While most churches do open their buildings to the

community for various events, I think building projects primarily benefit the people who already attend. We do it to have more comfortable, attractive, and convenient places for us to worship. I also think many of the professionally religious champion building projects because of what it potentially communicates about their leadership. Building projects give the appearance that there is a lot going on—that the leadership must be drawing more people and generating momentum. I've seen it in countries all over the world; the professionally religious use the size of their church buildings to broadcast how "big" a leader they want to be viewed as.

Not only should individual leaders question their motives about spending millions of dollars on building projects, but the leadership teams (elders, councils, deacons, and boards) should also ask themselves the same types of questions. Number goals and statements about being the "flagship" or the biggest church in the community can be veiled spiritual arrogance.

I can only imagine the amount of impact we could have in our communities and the world with the billions of dollars that are tied up in North American dirt, cement, and padded pews. And in an image, comfort, excess, and convenience-obsessed culture, it will take some very courageous servant leaders to cast a different vision of what the Church should otherwise be.

If yours is a church that works through the challenges of not having its own building, don't give up or give in to the idea that your people need brick and mortar to identify themselves as a church. If you're a part of the majority of churches that do own their own buildings, how can you profoundly minimize the resource-sucking effect that your building likely has on your priorities? Can you share the building with another congregation, or maybe two? Can you plant a new church in the community rather than build to expand? Would you even have the courage to help another church grow and encourage people to attend other congregations?

> ...I also don't see New Testament precedent for church-building projects commensurate with the resources we allocate to them.

I understand there are huge logistical challenges facing a church without a home building. I appreciate the rich spiritual traditions and symbols that exist in sacred places. But I also don't see New Testament precedent for church-building projects commensurate with the resources we allocate to them.

I don't believe that capital projects are always wrong. But I do think that they are often wrong, and we spend hundreds of millions of dollars on building projects for the wrong reasons. If Jesus was serious when He said, "Where your money is, there will your heart also be," (Matthew 6:21), the numbers tell us that for the North American church, our hearts are in our buildings.

journal on page 48

size does matter

Most of us know enough to say that size does not matter. And while we know it shouldn't matter, let's be honest, it actually does. We ask the size question in various ways. "So...how many attend your Sunday service now?" "What's your program attendance?" Or, "How many staff do you have?" "What's your annual budget?"

As soon as these kinds of questions are asked, our biggest task is to hide the wide-eyed look of insecurity to pretend we don't care about being compared to something. Some of the thoughts that can go through our heads include "Maybe I'll round up to make it sound better." "Maybe I'll give a range that includes the attendance at the Christmas Eve service." Depending on who is asking, maybe I'll say something about the good things happening in people's lives.

"Jesus knew that the Pharisees had heard that he was baptizing and making more disciples than John" (John 4:1). Evidently, the professionally religious really do care–even in Jesus day–about size. They are concerned about someone else in town getting more of the spiritual action than they get. They are trying hard to hide their indignation that another pastor seems to be attracting more people to his church. When another leader is asked to write the spiritual column in the local paper, for instance, the professionally religious think, "Why don't I get asked to do that?"

If we really believe we are not in competition with each other, if we mean what we say about the kingdom of God being more important than our individual church's growth, then is transfer growth really all that bad? The professionally religious feel a personal rejection when someone leaves their church or ministry and links arms with another. And yes, I do understand that these types of decisions affect deep relationships between leaders and their people. But how often is my reaction about the

> If we really believe we are not in competition with each other...then is transfer growth really all that bad?

potential loss of relationship, and how often is it about how it reflects badly on me when someone leaves my church and attends somewhere else?

Is my value as a leader directly related to quantifiable indicators of success such as achieving an attendance goal? Am I spending lots of time and emotional energy trying to fill seats? Do I feel personally rejected when people decide to attend somewhere else? Answering yes to any of these should cause me to question whether I'm building my kingdom or God's.

If we understood our role as servants as opposed to that of the professionally religious, we really wouldn't care about being compared to anyone or any other organization. No true servant that I know would take pride in knowing they have more work or more to look after than other servants. The role of competition in servanthood is of no use at all. The only thing a true servant takes joy in hearing is from the Master when He says, "Well done!"

journal on page 49

CHAPTER EIGHTEEN
the scariest thing Jesus said

In Jesus' first sermon, there are three verses that, for me, are the scariest things Jesus ever said. Apparently, it is possible to work for Him my whole life, have an incredibly effective and powerful ministry, change people's lives, be used by the power of the Holy Spirit, and still not spend eternity with Him.

Matthew 7:21-23
Not everyone who calls out to me, "Lord! Lord!" will enter the kingdom of heaven. Only those who actually do the will of my Father in heaven will enter. On judgment day many will say to me, "Lord! Lord! We prophesied in your name and cast out demons in your name and performed many miracles in your name." But I will reply, "I never knew you. Get away from me, you who break God's laws."

I would have thought that if I could speak for God, cast out demons, and perform miracles I would be pretty safe. I would assume that I would be pretty tight with God to have this kind of impact. God and I would have to be really close if I could walk around and perform miracles. Apparently not!

It is possible, and I would say even common, to work for Him but not know Him. It is one of my greatest struggles. We professionally religious can go a long time talking about Him without talking with Him. We can spend weeks speaking for Him without speaking to Him. We can fill up our time trying to live up to the expectations of many, all the while ignoring the One. The irony is that it's out of intimacy with God that we have any ability to reflect His likeness to the world so desperate for it.

> Is it possible, and I would say even common, to work for Him but not know Him?

A planning meeting is often easier than a prayer meeting. Reading a book about what another "super pastor" has done is often more tempting than soaking in the Word of God. Attending a conference is often easier to justify than getting away for a few days—just Him and me. I can't even comprehend the hell of that moment when, after living a life of powerful service, He could look at me and say, "Sorry...what was your name again?"

journal on page 50

CHAPTER NINETEEN
for whose benefit do i lead?

Be honest now. Why do you like to lead? What is it about
leading that motivates you to get up tomorrow and do it
again? Don't go immediately to the Sunday school answer.
Be real. What's your favorite part of being in charge of
something? For whose benefit do you lead?

Do you like to be the center of attention? Do you like to
control people and situations? Do you often feel the urge to
tell people what to do and how to do it? Do you often feel
the urge to find ways to remind people of what you know
or why you think you are right? Do you have a hard time not
saying "I told you so?"

Do you try to impress people with the eloquence of your
words or your prayers? Are you consumed and concerned

with the outward appearances of the success of your leadership? Do you feel the need to embellish stories that put your work in a positive light? Do you tend to exaggerate in order to manipulate the perceptions of people in your favor?

Do you lead for the benefit of those you serve, or do you lead for your own benefit?

Leaders who lead for others' benefit understand the burden of servant leadership. They understand that it often feels like more work than it's worth. They don't freak out when they're treated like servants, because that is what they are. They understand the load of leadership—the "I can't not do this" motivation for the sake of others.

I'm not saying that leadership should not be fun or fulfilling. We are more blessed when we give rather than when we receive. I'm completely convinced that being on the giving end of our gifts is more rewarding than being on the receiving end. What I am saying, however, is that those who answer yes to many of the questions above, those who lead for their own benefit, haven't discovered the servant in leadership.

There are many times I'd like to throw in this foot-washing towel I wear. Those who have discovered the servant in leadership would like to give it up some days.

It's usually in those days that I am reminded I'm not leading for my benefit, and that is good prevention from professional religion.

journal on page 51

a culture of "yes"

As I was reading the entire book of Matthew and looking over Jesus' interactions with the professionally religious, I was struck by what I can describe as a culture of "no." They felt their job was to say no to what God wanted to do unless they had a good reason to say yes. It seems that, along the way, the professionally religious had adopted a job description of managing an institution. The order of the day was to control people's behavior and actions by making sure they didn't break any rules. I'm sure for many, their motive was simply to protect the integrity of the religious law and maintain status quo.

Jesus, God in human form, didn't try to control. He guided, coached, communicated, asked probing questions, and caused people to think and change. Jesus influenced. He was a conduit, but He didn't control. Instead of managing to control, Jesus managed to lead. He didn't speak of an institution that needed to be protected or preserved, He led a movement that took the posture and created a culture of "yes." With the professionally religious, the people serve the institution and preserve the status quo. With Jesus, it was abundantly clear that the kingdom was there to serve out grace to the people.

Yes, we need to steward and manage the organizations that today represent the kingdom on Earth. However, managers of institutions have this proclivity to try to control people and situations. Ask yourself what culture dominates your staff, board, or decision-making structures; do you have a culture of "no" unless you have a good reason to say yes or a culture of "yes" unless you have a good reason to say no?

A culture of "yes" will create the necessary conditions for movements that transform lives and communities. A culture of "no" will immediately cause stagnation in any organization and will eventually result only in institutional monuments that only exist.

journal on page 52

CHAPTER TWENTY-ONE
contemporary legalism

Combine passion, focus, and zeal with only slightly-misappropriated leadership, and you can quickly have contemporary Pharisees and legalism. Any time we take our experiences and perspectives and turn them into formulas or expectations for other people, we take over the role of the Holy Spirit in the lives of other people...all the while using our interpretation of Scripture as justification. There is a razor-fine line between using the gift of prophecy, holding out the expectations of God, and becoming today's version of Pharisees, prescribing specifically how to live out God's expectations.

Any time we encounter persuasive and charismatic leaders who have applied Scripture to their context in a way that looks like a formula for success, it's very tempting to try to copy their extra-biblical actions in the same way they did. Out of a very right motive to be effective, we, unfortunately, try to find "the formula." And the moment we do that, we assume the role of the Holy Spirit. When something "works" for us, we then presume to prescribe how much money people should give, how people should use their time, how people should pray or worship, whom people should spend their time with, and the list could go on and on. You can hear a Pharisee a mile away by the constant criticism on their lips. The problem goes way back.

Matthew 23:1-4
Then Jesus said to the crowds and to his disciples, "The teachers of religious law and the Pharisees are the official interpreters of the law of Moses. So practice and obey whatever they tell you, but don't follow their example. For they don't practice what they teach. They crush people with unbearable religious demands and never lift a finger to ease the burden".

Do we, as leaders, trust the power of the Holy Spirit in the lives of followers? While God does want to use me in the lives of others, do I really think that He needs me to change the hearts of people who are not living the way I think they should live? Is that my job? Am I that full of pride that I think I can convince people to change? Am I so self-centered that I don't assume that the Holy Spirit is working in people on issues that He wants to change rather than behavior that I think they should change? Wouldn't I experience more freedom and avoid unnecessary stress if I trusted that the Holy Spirit is doing a fine job of changing people without my help and in my timeframe?

Can you imagine the burden-free joy of just being able to serve without the weight of the responsibility that comes with the idea that I am responsible for changing people?

journal on page 53

no leadership without real empathy

The decisions we make or conclusions we come to, even ones that seem automatic, are determined by the values we hold. Most times, we don't even think in terms of values or why we think what we think; we just act or react. We naturally apply our personal set of operating beliefs to our spheres of influence. Our personal value systems are products of our past and present significant experiences. They are formed by: what people expect of us, how we believe we are accepted, our interpretation of applying Scripture, avoiding painful circumstances, and re-experiencing things that bring us joy. And, because we are all formed completely differently by all of these factors, we naturally value certain things more than other people and exhibit different values in our day-to-day decisions and choices. We see and do things differently, often even when applying the same value system.

So as long as we surround ourselves with a bunch of followers who adopt or agree with as many of our values as possible, leadership is a fairly easy endeavor. And now to the real world...when we are forced to live and work with people from different experiences, upbringing, families, churches, cultures, and nations, leadership gets a lot messier. Therefore, an absolutely key competency for any leader who desires to have followers for any length of time is real, authentic empathy—the ability to genuinely put myself in other people's shoes, the ability to ask questions before making assumptions or drawing conclusions based on the differences I see. Because the less I know about what goes into a person's decision-making, the faster I am to impose my values and judge that person for not acting as I would. The faster I am to judge and come to generalized conclusions and assumptions about people, the faster and further I push people away from me, and they will never be able to live up to my expectations.

We place people in boxes. We can easily move into the expectation that our values and their application are the universal version. While there are universal and absolute values, there are many different applications of these values. While there are guiding principles, the reality is that life is ambiguous, and Scripture isn't meant to be prescriptive in all day-to-day decisions. However, it sure is tempting to use it to tell people how to live out their lives.

Once I have demonstrated real authentic empathy, once a person understands that he or she is safe without having to change first, only then have I earned the ability to influence a change.

journal on page 54

CHAPTER TWENTY-THREE

hypocrites and blind guides

I can't even imagine what it must have been like to hear the sting of Matthew 23 (see Introduction) the first time it was spoken. The followers of Jesus were drawing close to hear him, and the professionally religious were standing off near the back so as not to be confused with the followers. They were there to evaluate and pass judgment, not to hear and experience. This was a common scene painted by Matthew. Jesus consistently had two audiences: those who were there to experience and know and those who were there to judge and reject.

Mathew records Jesus calling the professionally religious hypocrites twelve times, and six times in chapter 23 alone. The word we translate as "hypocrite" in Matthew 23 was used to describe an actor, stage player, or a pretender. Jesus calls them out as religious actors and pretenders.

Jesus also called them "blind guides" in Matthew 23. The Greek root word for "blind" is also used in Scripture to describe blowing smoke or puffed up with pride and conceit. And the word for "guide" is also translated as a leader or teacher of the ignorant and inexperienced. He also calls them "blind fools" and the "offspring of serpents" who won't escape the judgment of hell: a clear comparison with the devil and his future.

The Pharisaical movement was born out of a very understandable desire to strictly follow God and His ways. Avoiding the repeat of all that led to the exile of the Jews and slavery in Babylon, an incredibly painful event in their history, their original mission was to keep God's people holy and preserve purity. These were good things and good reasons for their role in the spiritual life of God's people.

However, over time, they lost the point of their job. Instead of a focus to keep people in close relationship with God, they became focused on controlling behavior. To keep people as far away from sin as possible (a good thing), they built ridiculous rules and regulations on top of God's law and became the religious police (a bad thing). The behavior of God's people–not their relationship with God–became the focus. Another hallmark of professional religion is a focus on behavior over relationship. Right behavior flows from right relationship, not the other way around.

Puffed up by their moral superiority, the Pharisees also became an elite political force in Jewish society, which moved them even further away from servant leadership. They were characterized by strict legalism and fostered an unhealthy fear of God. As Jesus so clearly and repeatedly said, they were hypocrites. They were religious pretenders and spiritual actors. They were fake. The outside looked nice and shiny, but the inside was dead and decaying.

I have felt the same way many times in my professionally religious career; the outside is not reflecting the inside. When, because of the job, I feel the pressure to give the perception that I've got it all together spiritually. I get the idea that people expect leaders who look confident, sound like they've got all the answers, appear close to God, and have a spiritual walk that is worthy of being modeled. When these things don't describe my inner reality, but I constantly try and convey that they do, I become a pretender, an actor, a fake, a hypocrite. Pretenders turn people away from the real thing. Actors are only good for the show. No one will follow a fake for very long, and a hypocrite cannot run on empty.

Increasingly, people can smell a fake a mile away. They crave substance over form. They will have more confidence in a leader who is transparent about their messy inner life than one who pretends they are perfect. No one will trust a fake, and without trust, no one will follow a leader.

The antithesis of hypocrisy is when my outside life matches my inside life—when I stop trying to present an image of myself that doesn't reflect who I really am. That is when we stop acting. It takes incredible courage to let people see what's behind the mask. There is huge risk in letting people know your struggles, doubts, imperfections, and wounds. If you think that by presenting an image of spirituality you're preserving your job, you're actually losing your ministry.

journal on page 55

CHAPTER TWENTY-FOUR
critical and judgmental

There is a massive difference between "She works too hard" and "It seems to me that she works too hard." Or "He is irresponsible" and "I feel that he is being irresponsible." Or "They focus on the wrong thing" and "I don't understand how they are so focused on that." It's the difference between arrogance and humility—self-centeredness and other-centeredness. It's remarkable how many people make themselves the orientation to all knowledge or experiences.

Just stop and listen to yourself when you are talking about other people or groups, and see how many times your comments are black and white judgments. It usually happens when we are angry, gossiping, or venting (often a sterile name for gossip or slander). We make ourselves, our knowledge and values, the expected norm for everyone else and the filter through which we judge people.

We prejudge what we think are the motives or intentions of others. We make broad, oversimplified stereotypes in order to make sense of people who aren't like us. This tendency in all of us has given rise not only to common daily conflict in marriages and work places but also to the horrors of racism, ethnocentrism, sexism, and even war.

What does this mean for you and me? Here are a few examples of how we often judge people:

People who are brilliant at imposing order and structure? Bureaucratic.

People who shoot for excellence? Egotists.

People who anticipate and are always asking "What if?" Worriers.

People who are outgoing and social? Looking for attention.

People who are introspective? Arrogant loners.

People who are passionate about the future? Unrealistic.

People who can't wait to act? Impatient.

People who are great managers? Bureaucratic.

People who take risks? Reckless.

People who seek the opinions of others? Indecisive.

We evaluate other people's strengths through the filter of how they make us feel about ourselves and against our own strengths and weaknesses. The very qualities or actions in people we tend to so quickly criticize can be the very best things about them and their contributions to the team.

The professionally religious feel and act like it's their job to walk around and fix people, tell what they think the "truth" is (which is more often than not just their perspective), and point out what's wrong with everyone else. They are avoided, they are not emotionally safe, and they are not helpful at moving a group forward because they discourage, and therefore, hurt morale and momentum. They get a kick out of being feared. Their self-righteous disposition truncates any ability to impact lives through service.

> The professionally religious feel and act like it's their job to walk around and fix people.

People who are critical and judgmental are like porcupines, and everyone avoids porcupines for a very good reason.

journal on page 56

CHAPTER TWENTY-FIVE
territorialism in the kingdom

Although I do believe that the internal culture of the Church in North America is going through a cultural change for the better, territorialism and chiefdoms are very much still the accepted norm. For the most part, church (or para-church for that matter) is still seen as religious business rife with brands to protect, money to guard, competition to watch, market trends to be conferenced about, and customers to compete for. The most "successful" leaders are the ones with entrepreneurial gifts as opposed to shepherding gifts.

Molded by our commercial and well-oiled free market, the machine of Church continues to produce well-programmed constituents...but too seldom life change. And in addition to the world shaping the Church with its mold, I also believe that this territorialism is perpetuated by insecure spiritual leaders who base their self-worth on free-market metrics applied to "their" church. While most of us can wax eloquent about strategy and mission as the visible motivation, there is often an equally, sometimes more powerful inner self-centered motive at play.

Our glory.

The reality is that something very unhealthy inside of us can make a subtle switch when things start going well. Attendance, giving, outwardly successful programs, and numbers of baptisms and converts are all opportunities to feed the child in all of us that still needs value and validation. Is our commitment for excellence, results, change, etc., for the benefit of God's glory (and those we serve), or are we really more driven to be reliant on the praise of man for our value? Selflessness is not a destination but rather a

> Selflessness is not a destination but rather a journey of continuing to make sure that when people see me they increasingly recognize the face and heart of the Savior.

journey of continuing to make sure that when people see me they increasingly recognize the face and heart of the Savior.

journal on page 57

CHAPTER TWENTY-SIX
fighting over the how

I am constantly amazed at how, within the kingdom of God, we take our preferences about how the work should get done and make them universal expectations for everyone else. We never fight about whether or not we should worship, we fight about how we should worship. We never fight about whether or not we should preach the Word of God, we fight about how we should preach the Word of God. No one disputes that we should care for the poor, but there is much dispute about how we should care for the poor. No one would argue that we need to disciple our children, but many argue about how we should teach them.

> We prescribe our preferences and passions for everyone else.

It's so easy for me to love what I love so much that I expect others to love it also. We prescribe our preferences and passions for everyone else. And far too many of us have the arrogance, compelled by insecurity, to confidently add, "thus saith the Lord!" to our arguments.

While there are universal principles and commands for all Christ-followers to embrace, they are few. And I have yet to find universal methods that apply to all churches, cultures, and communities at all times. Let's be honest, our self-centeredness causes us to expect that everyone be "normal"...like us.

Mark 9:38-41

John said to Jesus, "Teacher, we saw someone using your name to cast out demons, but we told him to stop because he wasn't in our group." "Don't stop him!" Jesus said. "No one who performs a miracle in my name will soon be able to speak evil of me. Anyone who is not against us is for us."

Sounds like the start of a church split or a new denomination. Even Jesus' closest started to fight about the "how." Someone, not from their little group, started engaging in the work, but the disciples didn't have control. Jesus didn't care about how the work was getting done, he just wanted it done.

He wanted them to focus on the powerful reality that great things were happening, even if they didn't have control over how.

journal on page 58

the wheat in the chaff

At one point early in my ministry, I was on the receiving end of what I felt was some heavy criticism. The honeymoon was over; people had become familiar with me and I with them. I don't remember what the issue was at the time (which is probably indicative of its triviality), but I'm sure I wasn't doing enough of something, or I was doing too much of something else. In any case, I felt the criticism was unjustified, so I went to my boss and mentor to complain and hopefully gain a sympathetic ear. He was much too wise and caring to oblige my self-pity.

He listened and said two things that day which monumentally contributed to undoing some of my professionally religious underpinnings.

The first thing he said was, "There is always a little bit of wheat in the chaff that gets thrown at you, and your job right now is to find the wheat." The tendency of the professionally religious is a prideful defensiveness when we face criticism, constructive or otherwise. If we are tempted to base our self-worth on the approval of others, we can't handle the idea of being critiqued or evaluated. The professionally religious in Scripture sure couldn't stomach the idea of this son of a carpenter giving them advice or contradicting their wisdom. They were the professionals. They went to school for this. They were the ones with the titles and the office. The reaction to criticism is to then find a way to dismiss everything the person is telling us, especially if we question the motive of the one doing the critiquing. That is a huge mistake. We throw away the valuable wheat in the chaff.

> The tendency of the professionally religious is a prideful defensiveness when we face criticism, constructive or otherwise.

When I stop and think about the feedback I get from people (invited or not), some of it really is true. There is always a grain of truth or something about me that I need to learn. To miss those grains of wheat because of all of the chaff is to stop the work of the Holy Spirit that makes me more like Christ. And speaking of Jesus...

The second thing my boss said that day was, "If Jesus was crucified by the people He came to save, and He lived a perfect life, why do you expect to be treated any differently?" I didn't have much else to say at this point in our conversation. What else was there to say? If the Son of God was criticized, bullied, beaten up, and crucified by the people He had just spent three years loving, feeding, healing, and teaching, how could I expect to be treated any better? When we are criticized, we are in good company.

journal on page 59

the temptation to be relevant

For the next three chapters, I will be borrowing from Henri Nouwen. His book *"In The Name of Jesus,"* based on the temptation of Jesus, targets three temptations of the professionally religious. His short book, written more than twenty years ago, is one of the best works I've read in my study of leadership, and it deserves to surface again. I will simply do my best to summarize. I have identified other temptations that plague the professionally religious and will highlight those in following chapters.

Matthew 4:1-4
Then Jesus was led by the Spirit into the wilderness to be tempted there by the devil. For forty days and forty nights, he fasted and became very hungry. During that time the devil came and said to him, "If you are the Son of God, tell these

stones to become loaves of bread." But Jesus told him, "No! The Scriptures say, people do not live by bread alone, but by every word that comes from the mouth of God."

Nouwen makes the point that by being tempted to turn rocks into bread, Jesus is being tempted to be relevant. He is challenged by Satan to respond to the perceived need at that moment while ignoring the greater need.

The temptation to be relevant is as alluring now as it was when Jesus was tempted and when Nouwen wrote his book. In fact, being "relevant" seems to have become the mission of the Western church. Out of an appropriate desire to reach people in an increasingly secular culture, we mistakenly believe the way to do this is to become as relevant or as likable as possible. The professionally religious have embraced the premise that our efficacy is attained by relevance. We plan programs as though God needs us to make His message more palatable or current. We present as if He needs our charisma or our creativity. That's why so much time and money is spent on becoming well-liked by those outside the church–it's a way of drawing them inside.

This attractional model still grips the methods of the Western church, and it is a huge rut that cripples our growth. The common thoughts in the planning meetings of today's professionally religious are that it's our job to build attractive and welcoming buildings, and it's the people's job to fill them. It's the professional's job to devise well thought of programs and it's the people's job to have them well attended. It's our job put on a good show on Sunday mornings, and it's the people's job to invite their neighbor to church. And this is so often presented as the only real plan for the mission and vision of the church. We professionals will put on something relevant and you non-professionals will get bums in seats.

I see absolutely no biblical evidence or precedence for this model of ministry. Show me anywhere in the New Testament where a church cast a vision for a great new building or relevant program to invite unbelievers. Quite the opposite. People in New Testament churches met in homes and then were sent out into the world to engage with the broken, the sick, the lonely, and the needy. If anything, we were attracted to them first, not them to us. Today we've defined relevance with things like music, café seating, paint jobs, and coffee bars with the hope that a "cool place" will be enough to excite our people into bringing others. And when non-believers come to a cool place, maybe they will be interested in spiritual things because they will realize that we religious are not so weird. And, although some will be reached that way, it hardly sounds like the movement of power and transformation that the Church is capable of being.

I'm really thankful that God graciously uses so many expressions of outreach. Obviously, many people have come to Christ through all sorts of models. However, I don't think this is what He had in mind when He sent His disciples into the world to preach the gospel, heal the sick, and perform miracles. I don't think the idea was to make something so cool that people might then think church (and maybe God) was cool too. I think the idea was to "Live such good lives among the pagans that, though they accuse you of doing wrong, they may see your good deeds and glorify God on the day he visits us" (1 Peter 2:12 NIV).

Our mission isn't to be relevant. Our mission is to love God with all we are and love people as we want to be loved. And while I know that being relevant is touted as a means to that end, I think that relevance is more often a quest for likability, popularity, and being seen as successful to the world around us. I don't know if the current professionally religious have the courage to make the priority changes that would allow people to have the time and money to engage in the lives of non-believers.

Programs have to be run, and buildings have to be paid for, so it would take considerable vision and audacity for leaders to lead by example and meaningfully engage with people outside the church. I'm not talking about a one-time blitz of standing in a parking lot handing out free water. I'm talking about investing your time and treasure in the place where primarily non-believers live...even if it needs to be at the expense of another church program (one that truthfully just exists for those who are already there).

Let's stop hiding in the building and hoping people will show up so we can pat ourselves on the back and say we did "outreach." We don't need churches and organizations trying to get more creative in their efforts to attract more people by being relevant. Remember, we are not supposed to be attracting or drawing people to our church buildings. That

> Let's stop hiding in the building and hoping people will show up so we can pat ourselves on the back and say we did outreach.

was never the goal. We, on the other hand, are supposed to be drawing people to Jesus. They won't find Jesus in buildings or programs, no matter how relevant. They will find Him powerful in His people if His people are found.

journal on page 60

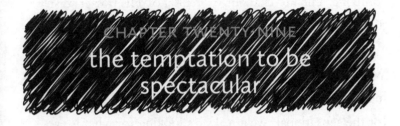

the temptation to be spectacular

"If only I could speak like that leader." "I wish I was as funny and witty as he is." "She is so creative and dynamic; I wish I could be like that." "If I had that church's budget, I could put on a show like that too and draw those kinds of numbers." Thoughts like these run through our minds all too often. But consider this situation:

Matthew 4:5-7

Then the devil took him to the holy city, Jerusalem, to the highest point of the Temple, and said, "If you are the Son of God, jump off! For the Scriptures say, 'He will order his angels to protect you. And they will hold you up with their hands so you won't even hurt your foot on a stone.'" Jesus responded, "The Scriptures also say, 'You must not test the

Lord your God.'"

Jesus didn't need to prove anything. He didn't need to impress anyone. He didn't need to put on a show in order to impact someone. The life-changing potential of His power wasn't displayed on stage.

We live in an age when people expect to be impressed. Our media and communication culture has created an obsession for the sensational. We are always looking for what is eye-catching and stunning. We flock to whatever the buzz or the trend currently is. We make decisions and will spend our time and money on what will give us the best entertainment value. It is getting harder and harder to catch people's attention.

Now, add to that our access to media and communication tools today. Spiritual leaders like never before have the potential to "wow" and entertain. From the time I've written this to the time you read it, new media will be created. If you had told me just ten years ago that I could make movies with my telephone and broadcast them to the world within minutes, I would have laughed at you.

All of this fuels the temptation to be spectacular, the false idea that our impact is conditional on our eye-candy. We think that if we are to draw a crowd, it will be because of our talent, creativity, showmanship, or even excellence. And here is where we are also susceptible to comparisons and jealousy. When we look across the spectrum of other churches and organizations and then think more disparagingly of our own work, we have yielded to this temptation.

God does equip leaders with public and even spectacular gifts; and when He does, He expects us to bring our best. Obviously incredibly gifted people can be incredibly effective and valuable in the Kingdom. But on the other hand, there are also people who try to function in gifts that are not theirs which results in ineffective to mediocre ministries. Both realities exist.

> Be freed by the truth that God doesn't need us to be spectacular in order to be effective.

The issue lies in our reliance on the gift rather than the Gift Giver.

Be freed by the truth that God doesn't need us to be spectacular in order to be effective. God is not restricted by the poverty of our resources; in fact, He shines through our weaknesses and limitations. The reality always humbles me that God doesn't need me, but He sure desires to use me. His wonder and awe-inspiring work is more often displayed when our glory is not competing with His.

journal on page 61

CHAPTER THIRTY

the temptation to be powerful

Matthew 4:8-10

Next the devil took him to the peak of a very high mountain and showed him all the kingdoms of the world and their glory. "I will give it all to you," he said, "If you will kneel down and worship me." "Get out of here, Satan," Jesus told him. "For the Scriptures say, 'You must worship the Lord your God and serve only him.'"

Wherever there are people there are politics, and it is no different in the world of the professionally religious. Many have this utopian expectation that we should be exempt, that our churches and organizations should be free from politics, and I understand why. The idea is correct. Servants don't pursue power. But in reality, we have far too many leaders that, under that veil of "growing the ministry," have given in to the temptation of power.

If you watch carefully, you can see the difference in leaders. Those who have given into the temptation to be powerful clamor and strive for more. They strive for recognition and titles. They always push toward expanding the scope of their territory rather than waiting for the next move to become obvious. Instead of waiting for the doors to open, they are constantly knocking, and at times, putting their shoulders into it.

I recognize the urgency of transforming lives just as much as anyone. But ill-timed initiatives that are motivated by egotistical leadership can do more damage than good. In the exciting conversations about expansion, church plants, growth, and strategic plans, open yourself up to being asked how much of your motivation is based on expanding your kingdom rather than His. The professionally religious are constantly looking for power, but servant leaders are given influence.

> Power can be both incredibly dangerous and incredibly effectual.

Power can be both incredibly dangerous and incredibly effectual. It's for whom we use it that paints a picture of whom we serve.

journal on page 62

the temptation of title

Matthew 23:7-11

They love to receive respectful greetings as they walk in the
marketplaces, and to be called "Rabbi." Don't let anyone call
you "Rabbi," for you have only one teacher, and all of you are
equal as brothers and sisters. And don't address anyone here
on earth as "father," for only God in heaven is your spiritual
Father. And don't let anyone call you "Teacher," for you have
only one teacher, the Messiah. The greatest among you must
be a servant. But those who exalt themselves will be humbled,
and those who humble themselves will be exalted.

Another temptation that is dealt with later in the great tirade
of Matthew 23 is the temptation of titles. What is it about
titles that feed our seemingly innate craving for superiority?
Even though Jesus eschewed the use of titles in the kingdom,

we keep on doing it, and we still place considerable value on professionally religious titles. None of the titles and prefixes used for the professionally religious throughout history have any basis in the Bible. It's all Church tradition. Jesus told us not to call each other "Teacher" or "Father." Could we also assume He would have included "Reverend," "Pastor," and "Bishop" in that same list?

What's even more headshaking is that the very next verse tells us that servants don't have titles. There is no order or rank among the servant classes. I've never heard of a head servant or a most high slave. Servants are not worthy of respect or due titles that communicate their honor or class. Again from Paul, "he emptied himself, he made himself nothing, taking the very nature of a servant" (Philippians 2:7).

> We like the honor and the ceremony because it lifts us above the common and makes us feel more valuable.

So why do we still rely on labels to give us our credibility, authority, or status as leaders? We like being separated from the rest. We like the honor and the ceremony because it lifts us above the common and makes us feel more valuable. I realize that titles give people context to understand our roles. I'm not suggesting that labels are not without practical value. This isn't what Jesus is getting at. He said the professionally religious in His day "loved" their titles. They were addicted to the superiority. Those of us with titles and degrees know the difference. I believe, deep down, we realize the difference between the practical value of how the labels communicate what our job is and the times when the peacock awakes in all of us.

journal on page 63

CHAPTER THIRTY-TWO

the temptation to control

One of the first signs that someone has the spiritual gift of leadership is a natural bent to want to control their environment and people in it. Watch kids on the playground. The kid that is talking the most and trying to control the other kids likely has the raw and undeveloped gift of leadership.

Given the public nature of leaders and the external nature of this temptation, it's pretty easy to spot control freaks. Controllers have a hard time not cutting people off or trying to grab the steering wheel in conversations. They like to remind people of their experience and why their opinion should be listened to or why it should carry more weight. They won't let issues go until people see things their way. They use words that portray issues often as black and white. Controllers operate best with right vs. wrong. They stereotype people and oversimplify complex issues to give the appearance that their perspective is the only one that should make sense. Controllers don't ask questions to clarify meaning or intentions; they make statements and tell other people what they should think. They avoid face-to-face conflict because they are afraid of the reality of other perspectives. They are much more comfortable to live within the reality of their own frame of reference, and they try to get everyone else to as well.

The professionally religious crave control over people. They want agreement. They take it personally when someone disagrees with their idea or position. They want order. Everyone needs to know his or her place, and more importantly, everyone needs to know who's in charge. They want approval. They like to manipulate because it is important to protect the way in which people think of them. They want power. It's through the perception of power that they can protect their position.

Servant leaders, instead, crave influence over control. They want dialogue and consensus. They are more fulfilled when people come to conclusions on their own. They create healthy disorder. There is more room for creativity when the body is working together and sharing ownership over the results. They don't need approval. They are secure in their role as a servant, and they know they cannot control what people think of them, so why bother? They want empowerment over power. They love the sidelines more than the spotlight. They are not hurt or annoyed by not being thought of or recognized. Servants have nothing to protect or promote. Servants don't feel devalued when things don't go their way or when they are not lauded.

It is much easier to see this tendency in other people before we see it in ourselves. Do we professionally religious have the courage to ask those closest to us if they see symptoms of control? Are we courageous enough to follow Jesus into the lifestyle of servanthood, making the daily decisions of dying to self and of not giving in to the temptation to control? If so, we then have to work for the change we seek by first picking up a towel and washing feet.

journal on page 64

the temptation of entitlement

At some point, something happened to David. The before picture is of a tender-hearted shepherd boy. He had a soft heart of worship, but he also had a fierce trust in how big and powerful his God was. The after picture is of a king who despite having as many wives as he wanted, felt he was entitled to this one more woman regardless of whom she was already married to or whose daughter she was. And that was just the start. Once it became complicated, David had her husband killed to try to cover up his sin. So again, before, David was the tender, soft-hearted shepherd boy who slew Goliath. After, he became the selfish, adulterator and murderer. How did this happen?

Success, titles, power, approval, control, (and wealth in

this case) all worked together to subtly and slowly change David's heart. Instead of letting God be his strength and supply, David came to a place of entitlement. One of the often-subtle side effects of positions of leadership is an ever-increasing condition of entitlement. We come to feel owed, or we gain certain rights and privileges because of our positions or titles that others don't have. The self-centered, entitled condition of our culture doesn't help either. We are, unfortunately, products of our societal environment.

Taking this attitude further into spiritual leadership, it becomes even more dangerous. The professionally religious often also take on an air of martyrdom or sacrifice. Because we assume all of these responsibilities, often without the same financial compensations as other leaders, we adopt a "poor me" attitude to our entitlement. It might look or sound spiritual, but it's a bad representation of the kingdom and the King.

I wrote the last sentence quite a while ago and have been watching the cursor blink for some time now. I went and got a cup of tea and came back. Then I had dinner and came back again. The reason? I can't figure out anything helpful or practical to write that could help reduce a penchant for entitlement among the professionally religious.

Let's look back to King David. If anyone needs motivation to think twice about giving in to entitlement, you can read about how that one moment of self-centeredness paled in comparison to the lives it destroyed and the turmoil that followed David. Yes, there was forgiveness, but there were also consequences from which many people would never recover. David's leadership, his household, and his spirit were never the same.

On the other hand, when our hearts and spirits stay one with God, when the level of our intimacy deepens, we feel we are less, and He is more. We grow to fully understand who's who and how un-entitled we are. We see everything as a blessing, and we see anything good as His doing.

> ...when our hearts and spirits stay one with God, when the level of our intimacy deepens, we feel we are less, and He is more.

It would have been much better for David–and everyone else in this tragic story–if he had taken a cold shower, picked up his stringed instrument that he played when he was a shepherd boy, and sang some of the songs he wrote that we still sing today.

journal on page 65

the temptation to be better

The temptation to be better is a more humble-looking version of the temptation to be spectacular, but maybe more dangerous. Sometimes it is called passion for excellence, and maybe it's that as well. The professionally religious like being thought of as better preachers, teachers, leaders, worship directors, or managers. They are secretly intimidated when someone says how much they loved the guest speaker last week. They want their program to appear better than whoever did it last year so people will see how much better they are as a director. They go overboard when they are involved or are responsible for an event because the better it is or, the better it looks, the better they will be thought of.

Being better at something isn't wrong. It is a matter of gifting, and God powerfully uses those He gifts. But wanting to be better, wanting recognition for being better, going overboard so people will think well of you over others, and wanting people to say or think that you're the best at something is incredibly dangerous for the kingdom of God. It's glory stealing, and that does not go over particularly well. While God obviously uses those He gifts, I think there is greater power to be seen in how He uses those who are weak.

> While God obviously uses those He gifts, I think there is greater power to be seen in how He uses those who are weak.

Even though the Midianite army was "too many to count," God reduced the size of Israel's army from ten thousand to three hundred to show them His power at work through their weakness. A shepherd boy slew the giant. God wanted Moses to speak to Pharaoh even though it appeared that he had a speech impediment. It was from jail that Joseph was promoted to prime minister. It is Rahab the prostitute listed in the Hall of Faith in Hebrews for helping the spies. The twelve disciples and later apostles were just common men with no religious training. And Jesus Himself was just a son of a carpenter from Nazareth.

God has this incredible knack for taking someone who is weak, someone who is average at something, and displaying His power in such a way that everyone knows who is really responsible. Here, there is no risk of pride. There is no chance that He will share his glory with someone who is gifted.

2 Corinthians 12:6-10
I don't want anyone to give me credit beyond what they can see in my life or hear in my message, even though I have received such wonderful revelations from God. So to keep me from becoming proud, I was given a thorn in my flesh, a messenger from Satan to torment me and keep me from becoming proud. Three different times I begged the Lord to take it away. Each time he said, "My grace is all you need. My power works best in weakness." So now I am glad to boast about my weaknesses, so that the power of Christ can work through me. That's why I take pleasure in my weaknesses, and in the insults, hardships, persecutions, and troubles that I suffer for Christ. For when I am weak, then I am strong.

God obviously goes so far as to inflict a weakness on

someone as strong as Paul to remind him from where his strength comes. Do we have enough room for that theology? To prevent someone obviously gifted from becoming proud, and risking a deflection on God's glory, Paul was inflicted with physical weakness to make it obvious from where his strength came.

As we strive for excellence, perfection, well-oiled organizations, and being better than, for whose purpose really do we strive to be better? Do we do it because our name is associated with it, and we care what people will think of us, or do we do it because His name is associated with it? And remember, He doesn't need us to make Him look better.

journal on page 66

CHAPTER THIRTY-FIVE

the temptation of busy

Why do we take the fifth commandment—rest—as a suggestion or a luxury? Breaking rest is listed right alongside of idolatry, murder, theft, and adultery. But somehow, we've been able to not only soften the Sabbath commandment, but we've even honored those who have the ability to live without it.

In Western society, we have given "busy" a place of recognition and respect. When I ask people how they are doing, the word "busy" so often comes back. Busy doesn't describe how we've been doing; it describes what we've been doing. The professionally religious today have fallen for society's definition of what a "hard worker" is. If our schedules are full, and we look busy, we are earning our keep; we are valuable, we are important, and we are needed.

Busy makes us feel good about ourselves, and it also justifies to others that we are "working." We wear busy as a badge of honor and pride. As a result, biblical Sabbath is often neglected by the professionally religious with very dangerous consequences.

Don't think I'm going to the opposite extreme again. Working hard is good. Commitment is biblical. There is lots of work to be done. And it's exactly for this reason that Sabbath is vital. Without biblical rest, we communicate that the work is all up to us. I say that my attendance at one more meeting is more important than paying attention to the King of the kingdom. How arrogant and delusional! Does God need me that badly? Will the purposes of the kingdom of heaven be thwarted forever if I say no to attending one more function? Am I really that important?

> Without biblical rest, we communicate that the work is all up to us.

If we professionally religious are committed to being an example to those we lead in service and commitment, why don't we have the same passion to be an example in Sabbath?

Sabbath is a statement of faith that it is His kingdom. It's an admission of dependency that we need Him regularly. Sabbath keeps us close to the source of power. The more we treat rest as an option, the less He uses us in His work.

When God rested on the seventh day, do you think it was because He needed a rest? Given the fact that He is all-powerful, I doubt it. He rested to model to us His intent for how and why we should stay close to the Giver of all life.

journal on page 67

CHAPTER THIRTY-SIX

the temptation of perpetual mediocrity

The local church is the only organization I know of that can fund mediocrity for an exceptionally long period. Think about it. What other organization or business can stagnate, not grow quantitatively or qualitatively, fight inwardly for decades, and still keep the doors open and the staff paid for generations?

I know talk of results is scary territory when you are talking about the kingdom of God. However, when I read the New Testament, results jump off the pages and leave me covetous of living in that time. So let's indulge in a short conversation about results in our day.

I hear lots of talk about the activity of the professionally religious, but little talk about kingdom results. I'm not talking about numbers. I'm talking about kingdom results. What is the Holy Spirit doing that indisputably demonstrates that God is alive and at work?

Instead, we talk a lot about the activity of the kingdom. We talk about programs and about what works and what doesn't. We give seminars, and now webinars, about activity. We give workshops about our work. It seems that people are happy to fund activity all day long and as long as we are busy with activity, all is well. But I so rarely hear people say, "'SO WHAT! What are the results of all of the church's activity? How do we know if God is busy and not just us?'"

> How do we know if God is busy and not just us?

One of the reasons that the culture of cold religion has gripped the professionally religious over the centuries is that its leaders get this idea that the institution exists for the religious activity. And it's right about then that the Holy Spirit starts pouring new wine into the old wineskins. If we professionally religious look around at our work and honestly don't see any of His work, it's then that we should drop to our knees and not get up until we all can say, "Ah...there He is!"

journal on page 68

CHAPTER THIRTY-SEVEN

doing no favors

There are few things that disturb me more than this principle of good leadership and relationships. Referring again to the religious leaders in Matthew 23, Jesus said they "crush people with unbearable religious demands," or, as another translation says, they "tie up heavy burdens and put them on other people's shoulders."

I see this in so many environments. We often think the harder we are on someone, the more we are doing them a favor. When people or situations are not behaving the way we want, we often become harder and harsher to get the right outcome. Spouses with each other, parents with their children, teachers with their students, employers with their employees, leaders with their people, and even pastors with their parishioners—all places I've seen people try to bring about change with a hammer. We get frustrated that we are not bringing about the change we want, so we assume that the problem must be with everyone else.

> We get frustrated that we are not bringing about the change we want, so we assume that the problem must be with everyone else.

We justify treating people that way with thoughts like "Well, they had it coming to them" or "they just need to learn." We think if we bring about harsh words or actions, we can teach people to act differently. That fear tactic only demonstrates our insecurity and our fear of failure in the relationship. If we need to be harder on people in order to bring about the change we wish to see in them, we failed in leadership a long time ago.

The professionally religious Jesus was speaking to had the same reputation. Instead of motivating people with the grace and love of God, they tried to prescribe how people should behave down to crushing detail. Instead of fostering a spiritually intimate environment, they became the religious police. They acted like it was their job to watch and wait for people to do wrong things and then pounce on them with corrective scorn.

When parents, teachers, friends, or employers hover, waiting to catch someone doing something wrong, they push their people away, losing any credibility or ability to influence them positively or speak into their lives. The same is true of the professionally religious. Western society has framed religious people as critical, judgmental, and better than anyone else. Could that be because of our chokehold on self-righteous prescriptions and formulas for how people should live their lives? Could that be because there are far too many of us running around telling people what not to do or reminding them of their mistakes?

Making people feel bad about themselves as a means to motivate them will either break or prevent a relationship, and at best, create superficial short-term behavior modification. On the other hand, creating emotionally safe environments is the only way to foster long-term change and the relationships through which we can influence that.

I've only ever seen people develop their character and change in the context of grace and safety–when they are not fearful of the consequences of failure. Most people know their weaknesses and know their need for growth. They just need favorable environments and people who will walk with them in spite of their weaknesses.

journal on page 69

heart-check questions for the professionally religious

Notwithstanding what self-absorbed motives we are trying to beat down in our hearts, a temptation of the professionally religious is to do our best to present the best spiritual image we can. We may tend to know the right things to say, but how consistently does saying the right thing reflect the real core value motives of our hearts? Here are some probing questions that have helped me dig out myself:

For whose benefit, really, do I lead or serve?

What is my first reaction when someone else is credited with my ideas or thoughts?

What is it that I secretly feel my experience or role entitles me to over anyone else?

Do I look for opportunities for people to see me as a servant?

Do I get defensive and aggressive when someone treats me like a servant?

Do I use self-deprivation as a tactic to publicly or inadvertently look for praise or affirmation while appearing to look humble?

Do I publicly withdraw in order to get people to look for me or pay attention to me?

Do I look for opportunities to exploit criticism in order to "play the victim" or build my camp?

Am I initially defensive when criticized, instead of humbly looking for the "nuggets" of personal and professional growth?

When someone is critical of me, regardless of motive, do I defend myself by thinking of some reason to invalidate the critique?

Do I attach my emotional wellbeing to praise, affirmation, or agreement of others?

How much of my need to be "up front" is driven by insecurities related to my sense of value?

Do I look for opportunities to abdicate responsibility, or pass off things I don't like to do, and call it "empowerment" versus helping people to be used by God, even at the risk of losing the spotlight?

Do I feel defensive when people do not agree with me or hold differing opinions about matters close to my heart?

When someone else is being praised, do I react by thinking of the weakness of that person to make me feel better about myself?

When someone close to me succeeds publicly, is it my first reaction to feel minimized or devalued?

Do I secretly compare my work or actions to that of others?

Do I "covet" the gifts and strengths of leaders who have more fame or resources than I?

Am I tempted to exaggerate stories or facts to cause people to think better of me or to be more persuasive?

Do I feel the need to subtly remind people of my experiences and knowledge in order to feel credible or competent to lead?

Is my pride or value in any way connected to the perpetuation of the clergy/laity distinction?

Do I want to be recognized as the expert, the fixer, or the rescuer?

Do I feel threatened by people who know things I don't?

Is my striving for excellence and achieving results more about people thinking well of me rather than God?

Am I threatened by a perceived loss of control or influence?

Am I jealous when others seem to be blessed in ways I am not or appear to have success I don't?

Do I feel the need to control people or situations to bring about favorable outcomes, or am I content to do my best to influence and then leave the results to God?

Am I trying to "fix" or change people for my benefit or comfort vs. God's glory and purposes?

Lastly...am I willing to ask three of the closest people to me to answer these questions honestly on my behalf?

journal on page 70

a servant leader's prayer

Lord...

Help me to be firm without being immovable.

Help me to take risks without being reckless.

Help me to be sensitive without being hypersensitive.

Help me to be confident without being arrogant.

Help me to be sure without thinking I can never be wrong.

Help me to empower others without abdicating my responsibilities.

Help me to be excellent without thinking I need to do it all myself.

Help me to take responsibility without taking ownership.

Help me to be wise without thinking I am wiser than anyone else.

Help me to first give the benefit of the doubt without prejudice that comes from stereotyping.

Help me to always show grace and understanding without criticism or judgment.

Help me to listen and understand without being naïve.

Help me to never speak negatively about others without first speaking to them.

Help me to serve with other leaders without comparing the results of my work to theirs.

Help me to be an example without the motive of being noticed as an example.

Help me to shut my mouth so I can be frustrated but without resorting to gossip and slander.

Help me gain Your perspective because there is always one I don't see.

Help me to know what you expect of me so I can care less about the expectations of others.

Help me to serve while knowing I will often be treated as a servant.

Help me to always be open to and learn from criticism regardless of the motive of the one giving it.

Help me to not subtly influence people to think better of me by influencing what they think of someone else.

Help me to handle "success" with humility and "failure" with grace and determination.

Most of all...so I can be this servant...empower me to seek Your face more and to better reflect Your image to the world so desperate to see it.

journal on page 71

CHAPTER FORTY
so—what now for the professionally religious?

There is no secret that I'm going to reveal or formula I'm going to prescribe. I'm not going to put forth a model or steps or phases or any suggestion of a quick fix. There is no program I've devised. I think the response is very simple.

Have you recognized yourself in the depictions or the temptations of the professionally religious? Are you also tired of the game of keeping the outside bright and shiny while the inside is rotting? Are you exhausted with the veneer you feel is necessitated because of the expectations? Do you feel desperate that you're running on empty but have to put on a show because of a paycheck? Do you feel most days that you're just holding onto a job?

The honest answer of yes to any of these questions is the start of leaving the ranks of the professionally religious. But, at least, be honest. If you like the ranks of the professionally religious and all that entails, if you enjoy the position, the titles, the honor, the separateness, the control, and the hierarchy, then have the courage to admit that, and don't talk the talk of servant leadership. You only cheapen it for those who do want to trade in the suites and the robes for the towel.

> Being demoted from king of the castle to the servant's quarters is a rough ride.

On the other hand, if you are finished with professional religion, I mean, really finished, only then can you embark on a new journey toward Jesus-modeled servant leadership. You can't dabble in both. Leaving the seats of honor, the positions of pride, and the comforts of the titles is hard. Going from the top to the bottom is costly and painful. Being demoted from king of the castle to the servant's quarters is a rough ride. Once you're hungry enough to make that choice, will the cost of humility be worth it?

Listen to how Paul describes his ride down the ladder:

Philippians 3:2-10a

Watch out for those dogs, those people who do evil, those mutilators who say you must be circumcised to be saved. For we who worship by the Spirit of God are the ones who are truly circumcised. We rely on what Christ Jesus has done for us. We put no confidence in human effort, though I could have confidence in my own effort if anyone could. Indeed, if others have reason for confidence in their own efforts, I have even more! I was circumcised when I was eight days old. I am a pure-blooded citizen of Israel and a member of the tribe of Benjamin–a real Hebrew if there ever was one! I was a member of the Pharisees, who demand the strictest obedience to the Jewish law. I was so zealous that I harshly persecuted the church. And as for righteousness, I obeyed the law without fault. I once thought these things were valuable, but now I consider them worthless because of what Christ has done. Yes, everything else is worthless when compared with the infinite value of knowing Christ Jesus my Lord. For his sake I have discarded everything else, counting it all as garbage, so that I could gain Christ and become one with him. I no longer count on my own righteousness through obeying the law; rather, I become righteous through faith in Christ. For God's way of making us right with himself depends on faith. I want to know Christ and experience the mighty power that raised him from the dead.

Those "dogs" that Paul refers to were the professionally religious, of whom he used to be the poster child. They went around saying that, in addition to Christ's work, the people must continue to observe the outward symbol of circumcision in order to be saved. Paul was emphatically making the point that there is nothing we can do to be saved. Our salvation is based on God's grace, provided by Christ on the cross, period. We can't earn it. We are simply and wonderfully adopted.

If anyone had the ability to earn his way into the kingdom of God, it was Paul. He makes a slam-dunk case that he was the most professional of the professionally religious. Circumcised, full-blooded Jew, clear lineage of the tribe of Benjamin, member of the Pharisees, obeyed the law without fault, and to top it off, he demonstrated his commitment by persecuting and even killing the followers of this sect leader named Jesus. He had all of the religious badges and stars you could get. However, he said it was all worthless. It meant nothing. It gave him no real spiritual advantage. In fact, it was a huge distraction from what really mattered. His religious superiority got in the way of the "infinite value of knowing

Jesus."

My translation reads that Paul calls his religious pedigree and background "garbage" compared to knowing Jesus. That's a sanitized way of saying it. The raw translation of the original language more accurately reads, "My religious training and background is as worthless as animal excrement, and I get rid of it so that I can have Christ and become one with him."

He wants to know Christ and His power. He doesn't want to be religious; he doesn't want to know about Christ. He wants to be intimate with Jesus. The word Paul uses when he says he wants to "know" Christ is a word that Jews would use when describing the physical and emotional intimacy between a husband and wife. Paul's passion is for intimacy with Jesus, and he came to see that religion was as worthless as dung.

My prayer is that you feel the same by now, that you're losing your appetite for professional religion. But I also hope that you are becoming hungry for intimacy with Jesus. The only prevention or way out of professional religion is knowing Christ and His power.

journal on page 72

Conclusion: Change

As I said at the outset, I am convinced that Jesus would say
the same hard things to the professionally religious today as
He did in His day. Everything currently being preached or
written about the ineffectiveness or irrelevance of the North
American Church comes down to ineffective and irrelevant
leadership. A group of people will only go as far as they see
their leaders go. As God so
aptly says in Hosea 4:9, "...what
the priests do, the people will
also do."

> ...what the priests do, the people will also do.

No amount of yelling and
screaming about a change will cause change. No matter how
many people are convinced that professional religion is alive
in today's spiritual leadership, unless those leaders are tired of
the status quo, the status quo is what will remain. The change
from a professionally religious institution to a movement
of Spirit-led risk takers and world changers is far more

massive and challenging than a brief treatment of behavior modification or "I'll try harder."

It is beyond the scope of this little book to treat all of the issues touched on by each of the chapters. But this book is about the need for dramatic conversion. I can't think of strong enough words to describe the transformation that's needed. I'm not suggesting that we need leaders with better leadership skills. I'm not saying we need to go about things differently. I'm saying that we need our spiritual leaders to be completely different, or we need completely different leaders.

> I'm saying that we need our spiritual leaders to be completely different, or we need completely different leaders.

I'm going to finish this book by looking at five different passages of Scripture. Each was spoken by five different leaders and to five different situations that needed change. They were spoken hundreds of years apart. But they all had the same message for what would create change in their situations. These Scriptures do not only speak to spiritual leaders. In fact, they all seem counterintuitive toward achieving a "fix" for professional religion. But if taken seriously, all would revive the Church to be what God intended the Church to be. I am fully convinced of this.

Psalm 46: When the World Is Falling Apart...Be Still

God is our refuge and strength, always ready to help in times of trouble.

So we will not fear when earthquakes come and the mountains crumble into the sea.

Let the oceans roar and foam. Let the mountains tremble as the waters surge!

A river brings joy to the city of our God, the sacred home of the Most High.

God dwells in that city; it cannot be destroyed. From the very break of day, God will protect it.

The nations are in chaos, and their kingdoms crumble! God's voice thunders, and the earth melts!

The LORD of Heaven's Armies is here among us; the God of Israel is our fortress.

Come, see the glorious works of the LORD: See how He brings destruction upon the world.

He causes wars to end throughout the earth. He breaks the bow and snaps the spear;

He burns the shields with fire.

 "Be still, and know that I am God! I will be honored by every nation. I will be honored throughout the world." The LORD of heaven's armies is here among us; the God of Israel is our fortress.

In Psalm 46, the world is falling apart, quite literally. Earthquakes are causing the mountains to crumble into the sea. The oceans are churning. The mountains, once symbols of strength and majesty, are exhibiting signs of fear and surrender. The nations on the earth are in chaos and uproar. The political powers are now powerless. The most stable physical element in our lives, the ground beneath our feet, is no longer a certainty.

The response? Well, my response would be to freak out. Everything steadfast is now no longer sure. The earth is the picture of everything solid, fixed, and never changing, and now it's all falling apart. In the middle of all of this anarchy and turmoil, God commands His people, "Be still. Know who I am." He says, "Calm down in the middle of the chaos." Even though it would feel natural to try and fix it, to try and put the world back together, and to try to take control of people and the elements around me, to paraphrase it even more He says, "Just relax, because I've got this."

This doesn't mean abdicate responsibility or justify apathy. Leaders obviously must be engaged with those we lead and the messy situations that come with people. What it does mean is to completely change our idea of whose problem this is to fix–to do away with the thought that we have the ability to change people or situations.

To "be still" (verse 10) is also translated "to drop it," "to relax," "to withdraw," "to let it go." And we can, because we know in whose hands we leave it.

When your world is falling apart, don't freak out. Be still.

Isaiah 40:28-31: When You're Tired...Wait
Have you never heard? Have you never understood?
The LORD is the everlasting God, the Creator of all the earth.
He never grows weak or weary. No one can measure the depths of His understanding.
He gives power to the weak and strength to the powerless.
Even youths will become weak and tired, and young men will fall in exhaustion. But those who trust in the LORD will find

new strength. They will soar high on wings like eagles. They will run and not grow weary. They will walk and not faint.

In a busy obsessed culture, our value is determined by how full our schedule is. This Western value also has a chokehold on the Church. Our churches often run like businesses, and their leaders function like CEOs. Unless the activity schedule is full, our value and our worth are questioned. Our propensity to program ourselves into effectiveness is increasingly leaving little time for what it is that really changes lives. And while there are so many facets of this reality that are dangerous, one of the many consequences is that it leaves leaders and followers exhausted and empty.

When leaders are physically exhausted and spiritually empty, their need to still be "on the job" contributes to the creation of professional religion. And whether you are spent and empty from professional religion or the rat race of life, Isaiah 40 has the most incredible and counter-culture solution. God says, "Wait."

If we are exhausted, we are told to wait. To wait is also translated "to hope," "to trust," "to expect," or "to lie in wait". I love that last one—to lie in wait. To stop the activity and lie down and wait in expectation for our God, who never grows tired or empty, to fill you and the situation that has you exhausted.

When you are tired, wait.

John 15:1-4: When There are No Results...Remain
I am the true grapevine, and my Father is the gardener. He cuts off every branch of mine that doesn't produce fruit, and he prunes the branches that do bear fruit so they will produce even more. You have already been pruned and purified by the message I have given you. Remain in me, and I will remain in you. For a branch cannot produce fruit if it is severed from the vine, and you cannot be fruitful unless you remain in me.

One of the most piercing questions someone can ask of a spiritual leader is "Where is the fruit in your ministry?" Not "Where is the activity of your ministry?" But rather, "Show me the fruit."

Are lives being changed? Are people being transformed? Are people becoming more like Jesus? Are relationships being healed? Are you seeing the fruit of the Spirit evidenced in people's lives? Are you seeing evidence of the Holy Spirit's power and presence in people around you?

If I am only busy and not fruitful, I've got some serious questions to ask about my relationship with Jesus. Apart from Him I can do nothing. For the professionally religious that should be a sobering statement. In verse 3 Jesus said, "He cuts off branches that do not produce fruit, because there is no life in these branches. They are useless and only good for the fire."

What do we do if there is no or very little fruit in our work? My first thought would be to take a seminar, read a book, go to a conference, or just work harder. Jesus said when there is no fruit, we are to remain in Him. To remain is to "abide", to "continue to be present", to "be held continually", to "remain as one". The life-changing results we all long to see in our ministries come when we are one with Jesus. Social transformation is the result of a changed spiritual condition.

Is there no fruit in your ministry? Then remain.

2 Corinthians 3:12-18: When You're Tired of Religion...See and Reflect

Since this new way gives us such confidence, we can be very bold. We are not like Moses, who put a veil over his face so the people of Israel would not see the glory, even though it was destined to fade away. But the people's minds were hardened, and to this day whenever the old covenant is being read, the same veil covers their minds so they cannot understand the truth. And this veil can be removed only by believing in Christ. Yes, even today when they read Moses' writings, their hearts are covered with that veil, and they do not understand.

But whenever someone turns to the Lord, the veil is taken away. For the Lord is the Spirit, and wherever the Spirit of the Lord is, there is freedom. So all of us who have had that veil removed can see and reflect the glory of the Lord. And the Lord—who is the Spirit—makes us more and more like him as we are changed into his glorious image.

Religion is complicated. Religion feels like a labyrinth of endless paths with a multitude of guides telling you how to get to the end. Religion carries with it the idea of people becoming better through ceremony and rules.

Thankfully, Paul tells us there is a better way. Instead of working so hard to adhere to commands and worn-out systems, we simply just turn to Jesus. We focus our attention and intention on our relationship with Christ. We spend time in His presence. We put into our lives whatever fosters intimacy with Him. When we turn to Jesus, the covering or barrier is taken away, and we have access to His radiance.

And the result? Listen to Paul again: "When we turn to the Lord...we see and reflect His glory...and we are changed into His glorious image." What a beautiful description of our faith. It can all be summarized by the words "see and reflect." Our job is to see Jesus—to focus intently on Him. And, as we do, we are changed into His likeness, and we then reflect that likeness to the world around us. We can't become like Jesus unless we become intimate with Him. We don't become like Him with ceremonies and laws, we become like Him by being with Him.

James 4: When There is Division, Jealousy, Entitlement, Self-Centeredness, Competition, Consumerism, and Pride...Come Close

What is causing the quarrels and fights among you? Don't they come from the evil desires at war within you? You want what you don't have, so you scheme and kill to get it. You are jealous of what others have, but you can't get it, so you fight and wage war to take it away from them. Yet you don't have what you want because you don't ask God for it. And even when you ask, you don't get it because your motives are all wrong—you want only what will give you pleasure.

You adulterers! Don't you realize that friendship with the world makes you an enemy of God? I say it again: If you want to be a friend of the world, you make yourself an enemy of God. What do you think the Scriptures mean when they say that the spirit God has placed within us is filled with envy? But he gives us even more grace to stand against such evil desires. As the Scriptures say, "God opposes the proud, but favors the humble."

So humble yourselves before God. Resist the devil, and he will flee from you. Come close to God, and God will come close to you.

Among a multitude of sins and self-centeredness, James presents one cure. Draw close. Self, and all it produces, melts away in God's presence.

There are books, seminars, groups, and programs designed to give people victory over any sin issue. Most of these focus on correcting wrong behavior. Sin doesn't go away because we point it out as "bad." We will not sin less because we are convinced of its revulsion. Self and sin will become more repulsive when we encounter more of God. It's the enjoyment of God that brings the dissatisfaction with sin.

James doesn't say, "Live the right life and God will come close to you." He says, "Come close to God, and he will come close to you." What freedom! We are released from the pressure of religion, the pressure of always trying to live right to garner God's approval.

Notice the common denominator for all five verses? They are not passive, but they are purposeful. None of them focuses on activity or on the situations that need change. These passages don't offer a formula, a strategy, or a model. They focus on intimacy with the Father. They all focus on relationship.

> Stop giving so much attention and emotional energy to that which you lead and be still, wait, remain, see and reflect, and draw near.

The message for the professionally religious is direct. Stop giving so much attention and emotional energy to that which you lead and be still, wait, remain, see and reflect, and draw near. Everything you need will flow from that: peace, perspective, power, strength, fruit, results, unity, humility, purity, and joy. The counteragent of professional religion is spiritual vibrancy. The less you pay attention to spiritual vibrancy the more you foster professional religion in your life, and worse, in the lives of those you lead.

Your church, your organization, your family, and your community do not need you to be more professional, more competent, more slick, or more dynamic. Your charisma won't grow your organization. Your sense of humor won't draw people to what they need. Your credentials won't be what inspires people or transforms their lives. The world desperately needs more little "Christs." What it doesn't need is more religious people.

John articulated the antithesis of professional religion so perfectly in his description of a life lived by love: "Dear friends, since God loves us that much, we surely ought to love each other. No one has ever seen God. But if we love each other, God lives in us, and His love is brought into full expression in us...and as we live in God, our love grows more perfect. So we will not be afraid on the day of judgment, but we can face him with confidence because we live like Jesus here in this world."

Other Books By This Author

Hungry For Life

Our vision will only be realized when selfless values are lived out by an ever increasing number of God's people. In this book, HFL founder and Executive Director Dave Blundell presents a concise summary of physical poverty in the developing world and spiritual poverty in the developed world. He then paints a biblical picture of a compassionate community of faith, comparing the contemporary Western Church against what it was intended to look like. The final section includes the core value changes necessary for the Church to rediscover its place as a relevant force of love and compassion.

Other Resources From Hungry For Life International

Shekinah Band:
What You Do With What You Know

This CD/DVD project is intended to inspire, serve and encourage the Church of Jesus Christ in its quest to address both spiritual and physical poverty around the globe.

Pockets of Change

Pockets of Change is about stories. Stories of transformed lives, of people and families and communities changed, of hope against insurmountable odds. This powerful and thought-provoking book will move you to want to be part of a global movement of compassion and justice.